AAT

Bookkeeping Controls
Level 2
Course Book
For assessments from
1 September 2016

First edition June 2016

ISBN 9781 4727 4809 6
ISBN (for internal use only) 9781 4727 4865 2

British Library Cataloguing-in-Publication Data
A catalogue record for this book is available from the British Library

Published by

BPP Learning Media Ltd
BPP House, Aldine Place
142-144 Uxbridge Road
London W12 8AA

www.bpp.com/learningmedia

Printed in the United Kingdom by Wheatons Exeter Ltd

Hennock Road
Marsh Barton
Exeter
EX2 8RP

Your learning materials, published by BPP Learning Media Ltd, are printed on paper obtained from traceable sustainable sources.

BPP
LEARNING MEDIA

Contents

Introduction to the course

Syllabus overview

This unit is about control accounts, journals and methods of payment. It takes students through reconciliation processes and the use of the journal to the stage of re-drafting the trial balance, following initial adjustments.

This unit builds on the knowledge and skills acquired from studying *Bookkeeping Transactions*. Studying *Bookkeeping Controls* and consolidating the double-entry bookkeeping skills gained in *Bookkeeping Transactions* will also provide an important foundation for the financial accounting units at Level 3 – *Advanced Bookkeeping* and *Final Accounts Preparation*.

Assessment type	Marking type	Duration of exam
Computer based unit assessment	Computer marked	2 hours

Learning outcomes	Weighting
1 Understand payment methods	5%
2 Understand controls in a bookkeeping system	5%
3 Use control accounts	20%
4 Use the journal	50%
5 Reconcile a bank statement with the cash book	20%
Total	**100%**

Assessment structure

2 hours duration

*Note that this is only a guideline as to what might come up. The format and content of each task may vary from what is listed below.

Competency is 70%

Your assessment will consist of 10 tasks.

Task	Expected content	Max marks	Chapter ref	Study complete
Task 1	**Payment methods** Demonstrate knowledge of the different payment methods used by organisations and show the impact payment methods have on the payer's bank balance. **Errors in the accounting records** Demonstrate knowledge of errors which are disclosed by trial balance and those which are not. Show that you can identify the type of error being illustrated (eg error of principle/commission etc).	12	Payment methods	
Task 2	**Payroll transactions** Record payroll transactions in the general ledger.	12	The journal	
Task 3	**Irrecoverable debts** Record journal entries to write off an irrecoverable debt. **Opening journal** Prepare the opening journal for a new business.	10	Preparing and reconciling control accounts The journal	
Task 4	**VAT control account** Record transactions in the VAT control account, and show whether money is owed to or due from the tax authorities.	10	Introduction to control accounts	

Task	Expected content	Max marks	Chapter ref	Study complete
Task 5	**Control account reconciliations** Demonstrate knowledge of the sales and purchases ledger control accounts, and perform a reconciliation with the ledger accounts. Show your knowledge of the purpose of control account reconciliations through short-form narrative requirements.	14	Introduction to control accounts / Preparing and reconciling control accounts	
Task 6	**Prepare a cash book** Check a bank statement and enter items into a cash book, as needed. Total and balance the cash book.	10	Bank reconciliations	
Task 7	**Bank reconciliation** Complete a bank reconciliation statement, using a cash book and bank statement. Show that the cash book and bank statement agree using the bank reconciliation statement.	14	Bank reconciliations	
Task 8	**Correcting errors** This task will test your ability to correct errors. You will be asked to: • Record the journal entries needed to remove incorrect entries • Include the journal entries needed to record the correct entry • Remove a suspense account balance	14	Errors and the trial balance	
Task 9	**Correcting errors** In this task you will record journal entries to correct errors. This may involve the use of T accounts.	10	Errors and the trial balance	

Task	Expected content	Max marks	Chapter ref	Study complete
Task 10	**Errors and the suspense account** This is likely to comprise several short requirements in which you are asked to: (a) Open a suspense account to balance the trial balance (b) Re-draft a trial balance (or an extract to a trial balance) following the correction of errors.	14	Errors and the trial balance	

Skills bank

Our experience of preparing students for this type of assessment suggests that to obtain competency, you will need to develop a number of key skills.

What do I need to know to do well in the assessment?

Bookkeeping controls is the second of the two financial accounting assessments at level two. It is designed to build on your knowledge of double entry and the other topics introduced in *Bookkeeping transactions.*

To be successful in the assessment you need to:

- Understand the different payment methods and the effect these methods have on the bank balance

- Understand the bookkeeping controls (including reconciliations, journals and control accounts)

- Be able to prepare control accounts

- Process journals

- Re-draft the trial balance following adjustments

- Perform a bank reconciliation

Assumed knowledge

The following topics were studied in *Bookkeeping transactions* and are also relevant to this assessment:

- **Double entry bookkeeping** – *Bookkeeping controls* is still largely a test of your double entry skills, although at this level, new accounting entries are introduced, such as payroll journals. This means it is vital that you are comfortable with the double entry studied at *Bookkeeping transactions* before we build on this knowledge.

- **Control accounts** – the sales ledger, purchases ledger and VAT control accounts were introduced in *Bookkeeping transactions*. They are studied in more detail in *Bookkeeping controls*, where control account reconciliations are also examined.

You can see that several topics that were introduced in *Bookkeeping transactions* that are now studied in more depth at *Bookkeeping controls*. The most important thing to do, though, is to consolidate your understanding of double entry bookkeeping before your *Bookkeeping controls* course starts.

Assessment style

In the assessment you will complete tasks by:

1   Entering narrative by selecting from drop down menus of narrative options known as **picklists**

2   Using **drag and drop** menus to enter narrative

3   Typing in numbers, known as **gapfill** entry

4   Entering **ticks**

5   Entering **dates** by selecting from a calendar

You must familiarise yourself with the style of the online questions and the AAT software before taking the assessment. As part of your revision, login to the **AAT website** and attempt their **online practice assessments**.

Introduction to the assessment

The question practice you do will prepare you for the format of tasks you will see in the *Bookkeeping controls* assessment. It is also useful to familiarise yourself with the introductory information you **may** be given at the start of the assessment. For example:

You have 2 hours to complete this assessment.

This assessment contains 10 tasks and you should attempt to complete every task.

Each task is independent. You will not need to refer to your answers to previous tasks.

Read every task carefully to make sure you understand what is required.

Where the date is relevant, it is given in the task data.

Both minus signs and brackets can be used to indicate negative numbers unless task instructions state otherwise

You must use a full stop to indicate a decimal point. For example, write 100.57 NOT 100,57 OR 100 57.

You may use a comma to indicate a number in the thousands, but you don't have to. For example, 10000 and 10,000 are both acceptable.

The tasks in this assessment are set in different business situations where the following apply:

- All businesses use a manual bookkeeping system.

- Double entry takes place in the general ledger. Individual accounts of trade receivables and trade payables are kept in the sales and purchases ledgers as subsidiary accounts.

- The cash book and petty cash book should be treated as part of the double entry system unless the task instructions say otherwise.

- The VAT rate is 20%.

---

1   As you revise, use the **BPP Passcards** to consolidate your knowledge. They are a pocket-sized revision tool, perfect for packing in that last-minute revision.

2   Attempt as many tasks as possible in the **Question Bank**. There are plenty of assessment-style tasks which are excellent preparation for the real assessment.

3   Always **check** through your own answers as you will in the real assessment, before looking at the solutions in the back of the Question Bank.

Key to icons

	Key term	A key definition which is important to be aware of for the assessment
	Formula to learn	A formula you will need to learn as it will not be provided in the assessment
	Formula provided	A formula which is provided within the assessment and generally available as a pop-up on screen
	Activity	An example which allows you to apply your knowledge to the technique covered in the Course Book. The solution is provided at the end of the chapter
	Illustration	A worked example which can be used to review and see how an assessment question could be answered
	Assessment focus point	A high priority point for the assessment
	Open book reference	Where use of an open book will be allowed for the assessment
	Real life examples	A practical real life scenario

AAT qualifications

The material in this book may support the following AAT qualifications:

AAT Foundation Certificate in Accounting Level 2, AAT Foundation Certificate in Accounting at SCQF Level 5 and Certificate: Accounting Technician (Level 3 AATSA)

Supplements

From time to time we may need to publish supplementary materials to one of our titles. This can be for a variety of reasons, from a small change in the AAT unit guidance to new legislation coming into effect between editions.

You should check our supplements page regularly for anything that may affect your learning materials. All supplements are available free of charge on our supplements page on our website at:

www.bpp.com/learning-media/about/students

Improving material and removing errors

There is a constant need to update and enhance our study materials in line with both regulatory changes and new insights into the assessments.

From our team of authors BPP appoints a subject expert to update and improve these materials for each new edition.

Their updated draft is subsequently technically checked by another author and from time to time non-technically checked by a proof reader.

We are very keen to remove as many numerical errors and narrative typos as we can but given the volume of detailed information being changed in a short space of time we know that a few errors will sometimes get through our net.

We apologise in advance for any inconvenience that an error might cause. We continue to look for new ways to improve these study materials and would welcome your suggestions. Please feel free to contact our AAT Head of Programme at nisarahmed@bpp.com if you have any suggestions for us.

Payment methods

1

Learning outcomes

Having studied this chapter, you will be able to:

1.1	Identify the appropriate use of different payment methods:
	• Cash
	• Cheque
	• Debit card
	• Credit card
	• Bank draft
	• Standing order
	• Direct debit
	• BACS direct credit
	• CHAPS (Clearing House Automated Payment System)
	• Faster payments
1.2	Identify the effect of different payment methods on the bank balance:
	• Reduce funds on the date of payment
	• Reduce funds at a later date
	• No effect

Assessment context

The assessment will test your understanding of the main payment methods available to businesses. You will also need to understand how these different payment methods affect the bank balance.

Qualification context

Payment methods are only examined in this unit. However, this topic provides useful background knowledge for the other units in the qualification.

Business context

All modern businesses use at least some of the many services offered by banks. In order to determine the most appropriate method of payment it's important to understand the effect payment methods have on the bank balance.

Chapter overview

Payment methods

Reduces bank balance on the date of withdrawal

- Cash withdrawn from the bank account
- Debit card
- Bank draft
- Standing order
- Direct debit
- BACS direct credit
- CHAPS (Clearing House Automated Payment System)
- Faster payments

Reduces bank balance at a later date

- Cheque
- Credit card

No effect on bank balance

- Cash withdrawn from the till

Introduction

Cash flow is crucial to a business's survival and if a business is to run efficiently, it must:

(a) Understand the different payment methods available to settle transactions
(b) Appreciate the effect different payment methods have on the bank balance

1 Banks

Businesses must ensure that money received from customers and other sources is paid into a bank account, so that the bank can hold and safeguard the money for them.

At regular intervals, a business's bank will send out a bank statement showing transactions on the bank account since the date of the last bank statement, and a final balance on the bank account. Many businesses also view their transactions and balances online.

You will be familiar with bank statements, however, it is useful to see a bank statement for a typical business:

	First National			
	11 High Street, Greenfield, GR5 2LL			
To: Jones & Co	**Account number**: 38291035			22 October 20XX
Date 20XX	**Details**	**Paid out £**	**Paid in £**	**Balance £**
17 Oct	Balance brought forward			1,595.23 C
18 Oct	Cheque no 003067	424.80		
	Cheque no 003069	122.60		1,047.83 C
19 Oct	DD Benham District Council	450.00		
	Counter credit		1,081.23	1,679.06 C
20 Oct	Cheque no 003073	1,480.20		
	Cheque no 003074	1,865.67		1,666.81 D
21 Oct	Counter credit		1,116.20	550.61 D
	Balance carried forward			550.61 D

You may have noticed something strange about the debit and credit terminology related to the daily balances on the bank statement.

- A positive balance on the account is shown as a credit
- An overdraft balance is shown as a debit

This is the opposite way round to the way in which debits and credits are treated in the bank account in the organisation's own books – money held by the business is a debit balance and an overdraft is a credit balance!

2 Payment methods

The main payment methods available to businesses are:

- Cash
- Cheque
- Debit card
- Credit card
- Bank draft
- Standing order
- Direct debit
- BACS direct credit
- CHAPS (Clearing House Automated Payment System)
- Faster payments

Assessment focus point

In the assessment you need to demonstrate knowledge of the different types of payment method by selecting the most appropriate method in a particular scenario. You will also be asked to show the impact the payment methods have on a business's bank balance.

2.1 Cash

Owing to the rise in electronic transactions, cash is becoming a less common method of payment for businesses. However, it is still used for low-value transactions.

If a business receives cash from customers, it must be counted before it can be banked. You need to determine how many of each type of coin or note you have, the value of each type and the total value.

The easiest way to do this is to make piles of coins or notes to a set value, say £5 or £1.

BPP
LEARNING MEDIA

Example: Paying-in slip (paying coins and notes into the bank)

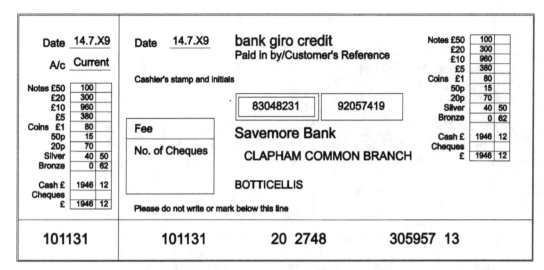

When cash is paid into the bank account (using a paying-in slip) it will appear as a 'counter credit' on the bank statement of the business receiving the money.

Effect of cash payments on the bank balance

When cash is withdrawn from the bank account, the bank balance is immediately reduced by the amount withdrawn.

However, if a payment is made from the cash till this will have no effect on the bank balance as the money is not in the bank account at the point the transaction occurs.

2.2 Cheques

Cheques are a reasonably common method of payment. They are a written order to the bank, signed by the bank's customer to pay a certain amount to another person or company.

There are three parties involved in a cheque:

Name	Detail
Drawee	The bank that has issued the cheque and will have to pay the cheque.
Payee	The person to whom the cheque is being paid (eg the supplier).
Drawer	The person who is writing and signing the cheque in order to make a payment (eg the customer).

When a cheque is prepared, the following details must be included:

- Name of payee
- Amount in words and figures
- Date
- Signature of an authorised person

Example: Cheque

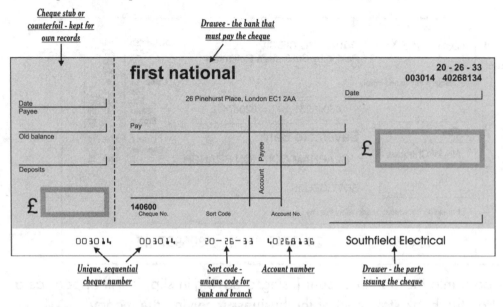

Cheque stub or counterfoil - kept for own records

Drawee - the bank that must pay the cheque

first national

26 Pinehurst Place, London EC1 2AA

20 - 26 - 33
003014 40268134

Date

Date
Payee

Pay

Old balance

£

Deposits

Payee

£

140600
Cheque No.

Account

Sort Code

Account No.

003014   003014   20-26-33   40268136   Southfield Electrical

Unique, sequential cheque number

Sort code - unique code for bank and branch

Account number

Drawer - the party issuing the cheque

If you write out a cheque, then the eventual outcome is that the money will be paid out of your bank account and into the account of the payee of the cheque. The cheque must be banked by the payee and then clear into their account before the money is available for use.

The clearing system is used for this process.

Generally, it takes around three working days for a cheque paid into a bank account to clear into that account. At this point, the funds can be drawn on by the recipient of the cheque.

When cheques are paid into a bank account (using a paying-in slip) they will appear as a 'counter credit' on the bank statement of the business receiving the money.

Dishonoured cheques

Some cheques may be dishonoured by the drawee because, for example, there are insufficient funds in the drawer's account. A dishonoured cheque is sent back to the payee so that payment can be pursued in some other way.

Effect of cheque payments on the bank balance

The payer's bank balance is reduced after the date of payment.

2.3 Debit card

A debit card is an electronic payment card that allows you to make transactions in person and remotely (by telephone and online). It takes payment directly from your bank account.

When a debit card is used to pay for a transaction, the amount of the sale is automatically debited from the customer's bank account and credited to the retailer's bank account.

There is no need to pay debit card 'receipts' into the bank as this is done at the point of sale.

Effect of debit card payments on the bank balance

A debit card payment reduces the payer's bank balance immediately.

2.4 Credit card

Credit cards are another common method of payment. A business can pay for goods and services by credit card at outlets that accept credit card payments.

The business is sent a credit card statement every month showing:

- All of the purchases on the credit card since the previous statement
- The total outstanding on the credit card
- The minimum payment required
- The date by which payment should reach the credit card company

The customer can then choose whether to pay off the full amount outstanding on the account or only part of it. Any unpaid outstanding amount will have interest charged on it, which will appear on the next credit card statement.

Effect of credit card payments on the bank balance

A credit card payment will not affect the payer's bank balance until the amount outstanding on the credit card is settled. Therefore, purchases do not have an immediate effect on the bank balance.

Activity 1: Effect payment methods have on the bank balance (part 1)

Identify the effect the different payment methods have on the bank balance.

Payment method	Reduce funds on the date of payment √	Reduce funds at a later date √
Cash withdrawal from bank account		
Cheque		
Debit card		
Credit card		

2.5 Bank draft

A bank draft is a non-cancellable cheque drawn on the bank rather than the customer's account.

The business will request a bank draft specifying the payee and the amount.

The bank will then take this amount (plus a fee) from the business's bank account and provide the bank draft. The bank draft will be sent to the supplier.

Payment via a bank draft is guaranteed and is usually used for large payments, especially where payment is overseas or in a foreign currency.

Effect of bank draft payments on the bank balance

Once the bank agrees to issue the bank draft, the individual/business making the payment must immediately transfer the amount of the draft (plus any applicable fees and charges) from their own account to the bank's account. Therefore, the bank balance is reduced at that point.

2.6 Standing order

A standing order is a method of making the same regular payment directly from a business's bank account to the bank account of a supplier or other third party. This is organised through the bank by filling in a standing order schedule (either paper or online).

Standing orders enable a business to make regular payments to the bank account of a third party. The standing order will be for a fixed amount.

Example: Standing order schedule

Standing order schedule		
To		
Please make the payments as detailed below and debit my account:		
Name of account to be debited		
Account number		
Payee details		
Name of payee		
Bank of payee		
Sort code of payee		
Account number of payee		
Amount of payment (in words)		£
Date of first payment		
Frequency of payment		
Continue payments until		
Signature		Date

Effect of standing orders on the bank balance

Payment by standing order reduces the payer's bank balance on the date the payment is made.

2.7 Direct debit

Direct debit is also a method of making a payment directly from the business's bank account to that of another party. However, with a direct debit payment:

(a)   The receiver initiates the payment and chooses the amount of each payment
(b)   The payments can vary in amount

As the payments can vary in amount, it is useful for regular, variable expenses such as telephone expenses.

To set up a direct debit the business must complete a direct debit mandate.

This instructs its bank to pay the amounts the receiver asks for, on the dates the receiver requests payment.

Example: Direct debit mandate

NATIONAL WATER

Please fill in the whole form including 'the official use' box using a ball point pen and send the form to us at the address below in the envelope provided. Please do not send this instruction direct to your bank.

National Water plc
PO Box 284
Donchurch
South Yorkshire
DN4 5PE

Name(s) of Account Holder(s)

Bank/Building Society account number

Branch Sort Code

Name and full postal address of your Bank or Building Society

To: The Manager   Bank/Building Society

Address

Postcode

Reference Number (as shown on your water services bill)

| 2 | 2 | 3 | 0 | 1 | 7 | 4 | 0 | 1 | 2 | 0 | 1 | 6 |

DIRECT Debit

Instruction to your Bank or Building Society to pay by Direct Debit

Originator's Identification Number

| 6 | 2 | 4 | 8 | 3 | 2 |

FOR NATIONAL WATER PLC OFFICIAL USE ONLY
This is not part of the instruction to your Bank or Building Society
To be completed by customer
Please tick required option:

☐ Annually   ☐ Half Yearly   ☐ Monthly April to January

☐ 1st of the month   ☐ 15th of the month

Instruction to your Bank or Building Society

Please pay National Water plc Direct Debits from the account detailed in this instruction subject to the safeguards assured by the Direct Debit Guarantee. I understand that this instruction may remain with National Water plc and if so, details will be passed electronically to my Bank/Building Society.

Signature(s)

Date

Banks and Building Societies may not accept Direct Debit instructions from some types of account

---

The Direct Debit Guarantee

DIRECT Debit

- This Guarantee is offered by all Banks and Building Societies that take part in the Direct Debit Scheme. The efficiency and security of the Scheme is monitored and protected by your own Bank or Building Society.

- If the amounts to be paid or the payment dates change National Water plc will notify you 10 days in advance of your account being debited or as otherwise agreed.

- If an error is made by National Water plc or your Bank or Building Society, you are guaranteed a full and immediate refund from your branch of the amount paid.

- You can cancel a Direct Debit at any time by writing to your Bank or Building Society. Please also send a copy of your letter to us.

Effect of direct debit payments on the bank balance

Payment by direct debit reduces the payer's bank balance on the date the payment is made.

Activity 2: Payment methods (part 1)

Match each situation with the most appropriate payment method by selecting from the picklist.

Situation	Payment method
Making a monthly payment for telephone expenses.	
Paying for items bought over the internet from a supplier used infrequently by the business.	
Making a regular rent payment to the landlord. The amount payable is fixed for two years.	

Picklist:
Cash
Cheque
Credit card
Direct debit
Standing order

2.8 BACS direct credit

A direct credit is a deposit of money by a payer directly into a payee's bank account. Direct credit payments are usually made electronically. This method may be used by businesses when they pay salaries and suppliers.

When making payments, details of each recipient's bank account and the amount to be paid are submitted to the BACS clearing centre. The payments are then taken directly from the business's bank account and paid in to each recipient's bank account.

Effect of BACS direct credit payments on the bank balance

Payment by direct credit reduces the payer's bank balance on the date the payment is made.

2.9 CHAPS (Clearing House Automated Payment System)

CHAPS transfer is an instruction by a business to its bank to move money to the recipient's account at another bank so that the funds are available the same working day.

Unlike a cheque, the funds transfer is performed instantaneously so there is no chance for the business to stop the payment, and the bank cannot refuse payment once it has been made, due to insufficient funds. CHAPS transfers are commonly used for large amounts such as transferring funds to solicitors for the purchase of property.

Effect of CHAPS payments on the bank balance

Payment by CHAPS reduces the payer's bank balance on the date the payment is made.

2.10 Faster payments

Most large banks and building societies in the UK now allow their customers to make small and medium-sized payments via the internet using the faster payments system.

This system enables customers to send same-day payments from their bank account to the recipient's bank account.

The business must follow various security procedures to access its bank account online, then enter the recipient's details and authorise the payment.

Usually the payment is deducted immediately from the business's account, and is available almost immediately in the recipient's account (around two hours).

Effect of faster payments on the bank balance

A faster payment reduces the business's bank balance on the date of payment.

Activity 3: Effect payment methods have on the bank balance (part 2)

Identify the effect the different payment methods have on the bank balance.

Payment method	Reduce funds on the date of payment √	No effect √
Standing order	√	√
Direct debit		√
Cash withdrawal from the till	√	
Faster payment	√	

Activity 4: Payment methods (part 2)

Match each situation with the most appropriate payment method by selecting from the picklist.

Situation	Payment method
Paying the monthly payroll to employees	*BACS*
Paying for goods required urgently. The goods are of relatively low value, however, the supplier requires immediate payment before they are despatched	*CHAPS*
Making a payment to acquire new business premises. The funds must be transferred to the seller the same working day	*Faster payment*

Picklist:

BACS direct credit
CHAPS
Direct debit
Faster payment
Standing order

Chapter summary

- There are many ways in which businesses can make payments to suppliers and employees. The method they choose will depend on the nature of the transaction and whether or not an immediate payment is required.

- Payment methods which reduce the bank balance on the date of payment:
  - Cash withdrawn from the bank account
  - Debit card
  - Bank draft
  - Standing order
  - Direct debit
  - BACS direct credit
  - CHAPS (Clearing House Automated Payment System)
  - Faster payments

- Payment methods which reduce the bank balance at a later date:
  - Cheque
  - Credit card

- Payment methods which have no effect on the bank balance:
  - Cash withdrawn from the till

Keywords

- **BACS direct credit:** A deposit of money by a payer directly into a payee's bank account

- **Bank draft:** Non-cancellable cheque drawn on the bank rather than the customer's account

- **Bank statement:** Shows payments into and out of the bank account since the date of the last bank statement and the closing balance on a certain date

- **CHAPS:** An instruction by the business to its bank to move a large amount of money to the recipient's account at another bank so the money is available the same working day

- **Cheque:** A customer's written order to their bank to pay a specified sum to a particular individual/organisation

- **Clearing system:** The system set up by the major banks to deal with the payment of cheques which means there is typically a delay of three business days between paying a cheque into an account and being able to access the money

- **Counter credit:** A term used on bank statements to refer to cash and cheques paid in to the business's bank account at the bank's counter

- **Credit card:** A card that allows the customer to purchase goods and services on credit now but gives them flexibility as to when they repay the credit card company

- **Debit card:** A card that allows the customer to purchase goods and services where the sale is automatically debited from the customer's bank account and credited to the supplier's bank account

- **Direct debit:** A method of making payments direct from the bank where payments are for variable amounts and/or varying time intervals

- **Dishonoured cheque:** A cheque that has not been paid as expected by the bank on which it is drawn

- **Drawee:** The bank that has issued the cheque and will have to pay the cheque

- **Drawer:** The person who is writing and signing the cheque in order to make a payment

- **Faster payments:** A system that allows customers to make small and medium-sized payments online almost instantaneously

- **Payee:** The person to whom the cheque is being paid

- **Paying-in slip:** A pre-printed document for paying cash and cheques into a bank account

- **Standing order:** A method of making the same regular payment directly from a business's bank account to the bank account of a supplier or other third party

Activity answers

Activity 1: Effect payment methods have on the bank balance (part 1)

Payment method	Reduce funds on the date of payment √	Reduce funds at a later date √
Cash withdrawal from bank account	√	
Cheque		√
Debit card	√	
Credit card		√

Activity 2: Payment methods (part 1)

Situation	Payment method
Making a monthly payment for telephone expenses.	Direct debit
Paying for items bought over the internet from a supplier used infrequently by the business.	Credit card
Making a regular rent payment to the landlord. The amount payable is fixed for two years.	Standing order

Activity 3: Effect payment methods have on the bank balance (part 2)

Payment method	Reduce funds on the date of payment √	No effect √
Standing order	√	
Direct debit	√	
Cash withdrawal from the till		√
Faster payment	√	

Activity 4: Payment methods (part 2)

Situation	Payment method
Paying the monthly payroll to employees.	BACS direct credit
Paying for goods required urgently. The goods are of relatively low value, however, the supplier requires immediate payment before they are despatched.	Faster payment
Making a payment to acquire new business premises. The funds must be transferred to the seller the same working day.	CHAPS

1 **Identify whether each of the statements below is true or false.**

Statement	True ✓	False ✓
A bank draft cannot be cancelled once it has been issued.		
Any customer who pays with a debit card is taking out a loan with its bank as a result.		

2 **Complete the following statements by selecting from the picklist below.**

Statement	Impact on bank account
When a payment is made using a debit card, the money leaves the bank account	
When a payment is made using a credit card, the money leaves the bank account	

Picklist:

at a later date
immediately

3 **Complete the following statements by selecting from the picklist below.**

Statement	Impact on bank account
When a payment is made using BACs direct credit, the money leaves the bank account	
When a payment is made using CHAPS, the money leaves the bank account	

Picklist:

at a later date
immediately

4 **Complete the following statements by selecting from the picklist below.**

Statement	Term
In respect of cheques, the person to whom the cheque is payable is the	
In respect of cheques, the person writing and signing the cheque in order to make the payment is the	
In respect of cheques, the bank who has issued the cheque and will have to pay the cheque (ie the customer's bank) is the	

Picklist:

drawee
drawer
payee

5 **Complete the following sentence.**

A		is a method of making the same regular payment for a fixed
amount directly from a business's bank account to the bank account of a supplier.		

Picklist:

direct debit
standing order

Bank reconciliations

2

Learning outcomes

Having studied this chapter, you will be able to:

2.2	**Identify the purpose of reconciliation** • Reasons for reconciling the bank statement with the cash book

5.1	**Locate differences between items on the bank statement and entries in the cash book**
	 • Recognise items on the bank statement but not in the cash book and recognise items in the cash book but not on the bank statement:
	    – Opening balance differences
	    – Bank interest paid/received
	    – Bank charges
	    – Automated payments/receipts
	    – Unpresented cheques
	    – Outstanding lodgements

5.2	**Use the bank statement to update the cash book**
	 • Make appropriate entries from the bank statement into the cash book:
	    – Bank interest paid/received
	    – Bank charges
	    – Automated payments/receipts
	 • Total and balance the cash book:
	    – Credit/debit balance carried down
	    – Credit/debit balance brought down

5.3	**Produce a bank reconciliation statement**
	 • Use appropriate items to complete a bank reconciliation statement:
	    – Closing bank statement credit balance
	    – Unpresented cheques
	    – Outstanding lodgements
	 • Check a bank statement has been correctly reconciled with a (debit) closing cash book balance

Assessment context

There are likely to be two tasks on this topic. In one task, you will be asked to update the cash book and in another, complete a bank reconciliation statement.

Qualification context

Bank reconciliations are also examined in the *Advanced bookkeeping* unit.

Business context

All businesses have bank accounts which must be reconciled with the cash book so the company owners know exactly how much cash the business has at a particular point in time (eg the month end).

Chapter overview

Due to:

- Timing differences
  - Unrecorded lodgements
  - Outstanding cheques
- Cash book needs to be updated

Introduction

This chapter is designed to enable you to reconcile the bank statement with the cash book and prepare a bank reconciliation statement.

The cash book is used to record the detailed transactions of receipts and payments into and out of the bank account. Cash is a very important asset for the business and the company directors must be able to see how much money the company has. As a security measure, they will want to agree the balance shown in the accounting records (prepared by the accountant) to the bank statement.

Bank statements provide an independent record of the balance on the bank account **but** this balance is unlikely to agree exactly to the cash book balance – therefore a reconciliation is required.

1 Differences between the cash book balance and the bank statement

Differences occur for two main reasons:

(a) **Timing differences**

When a business receives a cheque from a customer or sends a cheque to a supplier, it will update the cash book. This means the cash book balance includes this receipt or payment.

However, cheques will clear and appear on the bank statement at a later date, which results in a temporary difference in the balance per the cash book and the balance on the bank statement.

The main timing differences are:

- **Unrecorded lodgements** (money paid into the bank by the business but not yet appearing as a receipt on the bank statement)

- **Unpresented cheques** (cheques paid out by the business which have not yet appeared on the bank statement)

(b) **The cash book has not yet been updated to include items that already appear on the bank statements**

Typical examples include:

- Standing orders (SO)

- Direct debits (DD)

- BACS direct credits (for example, payments made to staff for salaries, monies received electronically from credit customers)

- Bank charges

- Interest (received or charged)

- Counter credit (cash and cheques paid into the business's bank account at the bank's counter by someone from the business)

Often, when a business receives the monthly bank statement they will then update the cash book to include these items.

2 Updating the cash book and performing a bank reconciliation

When updating the cash book and performing a bank reconciliation, the steps are as follows:

1. Compare the debit side of the cash book to the paid in amounts shown on the bank statement – for each paid in amount that agrees, tick* the item in both the cash book and the bank statement.

2. Compare the credit side of the cash book to the paid out amounts shown on the bank statement – for each paid out amount that agrees, tick the item in both the cash book and the bank statement.

3. Any unticked items on the bank statement are items that should have been entered into the cash book but have been omitted for some reason. Enter these into the cash book and then the adjusted balance on the cash book can be calculated as usual.

4. Finally, any unticked items in the cash book are timing differences – outstanding lodgements (debit side) and unpresented cheques (credit side) – that are used to reconcile the bank statement closing balance to the correct, adjusted cash book closing balance.

*In the AAT assessment, there is a highlighter function which enables you to 'tick' the items.

Illustration 1: Bank reconciliation

We will study the procedure for carrying out a bank reconciliation by looking at the cash book and bank statement for a sole trader, Dawn Fisher.

Below is a summary of the cash book of a sole trader, Dawn Fisher, for February.

Cash book – debit side

Date 20XX	Details	Bank £
2 Feb	Balance b/f	387.90
2 Feb	G Hollings	1,368.48
7 Feb	S Dancer	368.36
14 Feb	K C Ltd	2,004.37
20 Feb	F W Painter	856.09
26 Feb	J J Hammond	648.34
28 Feb	L Minns	257.50
Total		5,891.04

Note that Dawn pays in each cheque at her bank as it is received.

Cash book – credit side

Date 20XX	Details	Cheque number	Bank £
3 Feb	Long Associates	103567	1,007.46
5 Feb	Harland Bros	103568	524.71
5 Feb	L and P Timms	103569	1,035.76
8 Feb	Peter Thomas	103570	663.45
15 Feb	Gas Supplies	103571	480.50
20 Feb	F P Travel	103572	1,233.80
24 Feb	K Riley	103573	246.58
26 Feb	Farman Ltd	103574	103.64
Total			5,295.90

Dawn has just received her bank statement for the month of February.

First National
30 High Street, Benham, DR4 8TT

To: Dawn Fisher   Account number: 40268134   28 February 20XX

Date 20XX	Details	Paid out £	Paid in £	Balance £
1 Feb	Balance b/f			387.90 C
6 Feb	Counter credit		1,368.48	1,756.38 C
9 Feb	Cheque No 103568	524.71		1,231.67 C
11 Feb	Counter credit		368.36	
	Counter credit		208.34	
	Cheque No 103567	1,107.46		700.91 C
13 Feb	Cheque No 103570	663.45		37.46 C
18 Feb	Counter credit		2,004.37	
	SO – FC Property	400.00		1,641.83 C
19 Feb	Cheque No 103571	480.50		1,161.33 C
24 Feb	Counter credit		856.09	
	Cheque No 103569	1,035.76		981.66 C
28 Feb	Bank interest		4.84	986.50 C
28 Feb	Balance c/f			986.50 C

The bank reconciliation will now be prepared:

1. Compare the debit side of the cash book to the paid in amounts shown on the bank statement – for each paid in amount that agrees, tick the item in both the cash book and the bank statement.

Cash book – debit side (compare with paid in column on the bank statement)

Date 20XX	Details	Bank £	
2 Feb	Balance b/f	387.90	
2 Feb	G Hollings	1,368.48	✓
7 Feb	S Dancer	368.36	✓
14 Feb	K C Ltd	2,004.37	✓
20 Feb	F W Painter	856.09	✓
26 Feb	J J Hammond	648.34	
28 Feb	L Minns	257.50	
Total		5,891.04	

2. Compare the credit side of the cash book to the paid out amounts shown on the bank statement – for each paid out amount that agrees, tick the item in both the cash book and the bank statement.

Cash book – credit side (compare with paid out column on the bank statement)

Date 20XX	Details	Cheque number	Bank £	
3 Feb	Long Associates	103567	1,007.46	
5 Feb	Harland Bros	103568	524.71	✓
5 Feb	L and P Timms	103569	1,035.76	✓
8 Feb	Peter Thomas	103570	663.45	✓
15 Feb	Gas Supplies	103571	480.50	✓
20 Feb	F P Travel	103572	1,233.80	
24 Feb	K Riley	103573	246.58	
26 Feb	Farman Ltd	103574	103.64	
Total			5,295.90	

Bank statement (compare with cash book debit and credit sides)

Date 20XX	Details	Paid out £	Paid in £	Balance £
1 Feb	Balance b/f			387.90 C
6 Feb	Counter credit		1,368.48✓	1,756.38 C
9 Feb	Cheque No 103568	524.71✓		1,231.67 C
11 Feb	Counter credit		368.36✓	
	Counter credit		208.34	
	Cheque No 103567	1,107.46		700.91 C
13 Feb	Cheque No 103570	663.45✓		37.46 C
18 Feb	Counter credit		2,004.37✓	
	SO – FC Property	400.00		1,641.83 C
19 Feb	Cheque No 103571	480.50✓		1,161.33 C
24 Feb	Counter credit		856.09✓	
	Cheque No 103569	1,035.76✓		981.66 C
28 Feb	Bank interest		4.84	986.50 C
28 Feb	Balance c/f			986.50 C
D = Debit, C = Credit				

3. Any unticked items on the bank statement must be entered into the cash book.

Paid in amounts

- The counter credit of £208.34 on 11 February has not been recorded in the debit side of the cash book, so this must be corrected.

- On 28 February an amount of £4.84 bank interest was paid in to the account by the bank – this must be entered into the debit side of the cash book.

Paid out amounts

- Cheque number 103567 has been recorded in the credit side of the cash book as £1,007.46 whereas the bank statement shows it as an amount of £1,107.46. The cash book must be adjusted by including an extra £100 in the credit side.

- The standing order of £400.00 on 18 February has not been recorded in the credit side of the cash book, so it must be corrected.

Tick the items as they are written in to tie up with the bank statement and calculate the adjusted balance on the cash book. You'll find that the debit side total is higher than the credit side total, giving a balance c/d on the credit side of £308.32.

In preparation for step 4:

The items that remain **unticked** in the cash book are timing differences that will appear on the bank reconciliation.

For learning purposes, in the illustration below these items are marked in the cash book with an R (for 'reconciling').

Cash book – debit side

Date 20XX	Details	Bank £	
2 Feb	Balance b/f	387.90	
2 Feb	G Hollings	1,368.48	✓
7 Feb	S Dancer	368.36	✓
14 Feb	K C Ltd	2,004.37	✓
20 Feb	F W Painter	856.09	✓
26 Feb	J J Hammond	648.34	R
28 Feb	L Minns	257.50	R
11 Feb	**Counter credit**	**208.34**	✓
28 Feb	**Bank interest received**	**4.84**	✓
Total		6,104.22	

Cash book – credit side

Date 20XX	Details	Cheque number	Bank £	
3 Feb	Long Associates	103567	1,007.46	✓
5 Feb	Harland Bros	103568	524.71	✓
5 Feb	L and P Timms	103569	1,035.76	✓
8 Feb	Peter Thomas	103570	663.45	✓
15 Feb	Gas Supplies	103571	480.50	✓
20 Feb	F P Travel	103572	1,233.80	R
24 Feb	K Riley	103573	246.58	R
26 Feb	Farman Ltd	103574	103.64	R
11 Feb	**Correction of cheque**	**103567**	**100.00**	✓
18 Feb	**FC Property**	**SO**	**400.00**	✓
28 Feb	Balance c/d		308.32	*
Total			6,104.22	

4. Finally, any unticked items in the cash book are timing differences – outstanding lodgements (debit side) and unpresented cheques (credit side) – that are used to reconcile the bank statement closing balance to the correct, adjusted cash book closing balance (*calculated above as £308.32).

Bank reconciliation statement at 28 February 20XX

Bank reconciliation statement	£
Balance per bank statement	986.50
Add outstanding lodgements (from debit side)	
J J Hammond	648.34
L Minns	257.50
Total to add	905.84
Less unpresented cheques (from credit side)	
F P Travel	1,233.80
K Riley	246.58
Farman Ltd	103.64
Total to subtract	1,584.02
Balance as per correct, adjusted cash book	308.32

The bank statement and the cash book have now been reconciled and the figure that will appear in the trial balance for the bank account is the correct, adjusted cash book balance of £308.32.

3 Opening balances on the cash book and bank statement

In the illustration you may have noted that the opening balance (balance b/f) on the cash book was the same as that on the bank statement. This is because there were no unpresented cheques or outstanding lodgements at the end of the previous period.

This will not always be the case. If there were timing differences at the end of the previous period, they would have been included on the bank reconciliation statement at that date.

In the real world, when comparing this period's bank statement and cash book, you therefore need to have the previous period's bank reconciliation statement to hand in order to tick off last period's timing differences when they appear on the bank statement in this period.

In the exam this would be a minor element of a bank reconciliation question. You would need to:

1.   Identify whether the opening balance (balance b/f) on the cash book is different to that of the bank statement; the difference will relate to an item that appears on the bank statement for the current period.

2. Note this item on scrap paper. You do not need to include it in your exam solution, ie it should **not** be included in the cash book for the current period (as it would have been included in the cash book in the prior period).

Activity 1: Bank reconciliation – Bike Business

Bike Business received the following bank statement for September.

Date 20XX	Details	Paid out £	Paid in £	Balance £	
01 Sept	Balance b/f			10,879	C
06 Sept	Cheque 3456	2,960		7,919	C
12 Sept	Cheque 3457	4,900		3,019	C
13 Sept	Bank interest		60	3,079	C
13 Sept	Cheque 3449	1,300		1,779	C
18 Sept	Direct Debit – Elec Ltd	650		1,129	C
19 Sept	Cheque 3458	1,000		129	C
21 Sept	Counter credit – PWG Ltd		6,850	6,979	C
25 Sept	Bank charges	50		6,929	C
25 Sept	Direct Debit – FRD Ltd	297		6,632	C
29 Sept	Counter credit – ESD Ltd		450	7,082	C
30 Sept	Cheque 3459	2,700		4,382	C
D = Debit, C = Credit					

The cash book as at 30 September is shown below.

Cash book

Date 20XX	Details	Bank £	Date 20XX	Cheque number	Details	Bank £
01 Sept	Balance b/f	9,579	02 Sept	3456	QSH Ltd	2,960 ✓
21 Sept	PWG Ltd	6,850 ✓	08 Sept	3457	TGM Ltd	4,900 ✓
29 Sept	WTY Ltd	(590)	15 Sept	3458	FTJ Ltd	1,000 ✓
		60	18 Sept	DD	Elec Ltd	650 ✓
		450	24 Sept	3459	YHL Ltd	2,700 ✓
			30 Sept	3460	WMB Ltd	(760)
						50
						297
					CD	4212
		17529				17529
	b/d	4212				

13317

Picklist:

Balance b/d
Balance c/d
Bank charges
Bank interest
Direct debit
ESD Ltd
FRD Ltd
Standing order

Bank reconciliation statement	£
Balance per bank statement	4382
Add:	
	590
Total to add	
Less:	
	760
Total to subtract	
Balance as per cash book	4212

Picklist:

WMB Ltd

WTY Ltd

Required

(a) Check the items on the bank statement against the items in the cash book.

(b) Enter any items into the cash book as needed.

(c) Total the cash book and clearly show the balance carried down at 30 September __and__ brought down at 1 October.

(d) Identify the TWO transactions that are included in the cash book but missing from the bank statement and complete the bank reconciliation statement below as at 30 September.

4 Assessment tasks

Having looked at an illustration and activity, we will now consider assessment style tasks.

Assessment focus point

In the assessment, bank reconciliations will be split across two tasks. It is likely that the tasks will be structured as follows:

- One task – check the bank statement against the cash book and enter transactions in the cash book as needed; show the cash book balance c/d and b/d.

- Another task – review the cash book and complete a bank reconciliation statement; check that the cash book and bank statement have been correctly reconciled.

To be successful in these types of tasks you need a methodical approach. Make sure you identify the items that already appear in the cash book and bank statement. You can then focus on the remaining items.

A word of warning

Remember, as we saw in Chapter 1, the bank statement shows the balance from the bank's point of view, whereas the cash book is from the business's point of view.

Therefore, should a task state that the bank account is in credit, then this means that there is a **debit** balance in the business's records.

Conversely, should a question state that the bank account balance is overdrawn, then there is a **credit** balance in the business's records.

Activity 2: Updating the cash book

The bank statement and cash book for November are shown below.

Required

Check the bank statement against the cash book and enter:

- **Any transactions into the cash book as needed**
- **The cash book balance carried down at 30 November and brought down at 1 December**

Bank statement

Date 20XX	Details	Paid out £	Paid in £	Balance £	
02 Nov	Balance b/f			7,890	C
05 Nov	Cheque 7823	980		6,910	C
07 Nov	Cheque 7824	4,654		2,256	C
10 Nov	Bank interest	125		2,131	C
11 Nov	Cheque 7818	230		1,901	C
18 Nov	Counter credit – MPV Ltd		2,780	4,681	C
20 Nov	Cheque 7825	650		4,031	C
24 Nov	Standing Order – A Motor Co	500		3,531	C
25 Nov	Cheque 7826	410		3,121	C
25 Nov	Direct Debit – SAO Ltd	730		2,391	C
28 Nov	Counter credit – WD Ltd		476	2,867	C
30 Nov	Bank charges	75		2,792	C
D = Debit, C = Credit					

The cash book as at 30 November is shown below.

Cash book

Date 20XX	Details	Bank £	Date 20XX	Cheque number	Details	Bank £
01 Nov	Balance b/f	7,660 ✓	01 Nov	7823	RFT Ltd	980 ✓
18 Nov	MPV Ltd	2,780 ✓	02 Nov	7824	JGB Ltd	4,654 ✓
28 Nov	NON Ltd	(420)	15 Nov	7825	DER Ltd	650 ✓
		476	20 Nov	7826	WTR Ltd	410 ✓
			25 Nov	DD	SAO Ltd	730 ✓
			28 Nov	7827	REW Ltd	(147)
			30 Nov	7828	YLK Ltd	(589)
						125
						500
						75
					c/d	2476
		11336				11336

Picklist: b/d 2476

A Motor Co
Balance b/d
Balance c/d
Bank charges
Bank interest
Direct debit
Standing order
WD Ltd

2792 + 420 − (147 + 589) = 2476

Activity 3: Bank reconciliation statement

Below is the bank statement for June.

Bank statement

Date 20XX	Details	Paid out £	Paid in £	Balance £	
01 June	Balance b/f			385	D
07 June	Counter credit – PKL Ltd		4,000	3,615	C
08 June	Cheque 007303	250		3,365	C
08 June	Cheque 007315	483		2,882	C
14 June	Cheque 007316	2,165		717	C
15 June	Cheque 007317	1,233		516	D
20 June	Direct Debit Hampton CC	135		651	D
20 June	Direct Debit Motor Mania	177		828	D
21 June	Counter credit – Bissell & Co		2,500	1,672	C
22 June	Bank charges	44		1,628	C
22 June	Bank interest		3	1,631	C
D = Debit, C = Credit					

The cash book and bank reconciliation statement for June have not yet been finalised.

Cash book

Date 20XX	Details	Bank £	Date 20XX	Cheque number	Details	Bank £
15 June	PKL Ltd	4,000 ✓	01 June		Balance b/f	635 ✓
20 June	Beaker plc	(3,245)	01 June	07315	Abby Photos	483 ✓
21 June	Bissell & Co	2,500 ✓	06 June	07316	LTL Ltd	2,165 ✓
22 June	Gilchrist Ltd	(2,416)	06 June	07317	Retro Frames	1,233 ✓
22 June	Bank interest	3 ✓	22 June	07318	Tonks & Co	(1,020)
			22 June	07319	Taylor Agencies	(547)
			20 June	DD	Hampton CC	135 ✓
			20 June	DD	Motor Mania	177 ✓
			22 June		Bank charges	44 ✓

(handwritten: 12 164 / b/d 5725 ... 6439 / dd 5725)

Required

Identify the FOUR transactions that are included in the cash book but missing from the bank statement and complete the bank reconciliation statement below as at 22 June.

Do not enter figures with minus signs or brackets in this task. Do not make any entries in the shaded boxes.

Bank reconciliation statement	£
Balance per bank statement	1631
Add:	
3245 + 2416	5661
Total to add	
Less:	
1020 + 547	1567
Total to subtract	
Balance as per cash book	5725

Picklist:

Abby Photos
Beaker plc
Bissell & Co
Direct Debit
Gilchrist Ltd
Hampton CC
LTL Ltd
Motor Mania
PKL Ltd
Retro Frames
Taylor Agencies
Tonks & Co

(b) Refer to the cash book in (a) and check that the bank statement has been correctly reconciled by calculating:

- **The balance carried down**

- **The total of each of the bank columns after the balance carried down has been recorded**

Balance carried down £	Bank column totals £
5725	5725

Chapter summary

- To ensure the accuracy of the cash book, it must be checked at regular intervals to bank statements received.

- Differences between the cash book balance and the bank statement arise due to timing differences (mainly outstanding lodgements and unpresented cheques) and also if the cash book has not yet been updated to include items that only appear on the bank statement.

- When updating the cash book and performing a bank reconciliation, the steps are as follows:

  1. Compare the debit side of the cash book to the paid in amounts shown on the bank statement – for each paid in amount that agrees, tick the item in both the cash book and the bank statement.

  2. Compare the credit side of the cash book to the paid out amounts shown on the bank statement – for each paid out amount that agrees, tick the item in both the cash book and the bank statement.

  3. Any unticked items on the bank statement (other than errors made by the bank) are items that should have been entered into the cash book but have been omitted for some reason. Enter these into the cash book and then the adjusted balance on the cash book can be calculated as usual.

  4. Finally, any unticked items in the cash book are timing differences – outstanding lodgements (debit side) and unpresented cheques (credit side) – that are used to reconcile the bank statement closing balance to the correct, adjusted cash book closing balance.

- The closing balance on the bank statement is reconciled to the correct, adjusted closing cash book balance in the bank reconciliation statement.

Keywords

- **Bank reconciliation statement:** A statement reconciling the bank statement balance on a given date to the correct, adjusted cash book balance on the same date

- **Bank statement:** Shows payments into and out of the bank account since the date of the last bank statement and the balance at a point in time

- **Outstanding lodgements:** Cheques that have been received and recorded on the debit side of the cash book but do not yet appear on the bank statement

- **Overdraft:** This is where the business effectively owes the bank money – it appears as a debit balance in the bank statement and a credit balance in the cash book

- **Timing differences:** The reasons why the bank statement balance rarely agrees with the balance on the cash book, as receipts and payments recorded in the cash book appear later on the bank statement due to, for example, how the clearing system operates

- **Unpresented cheques:** Cheque payments that have been recorded in the credit side of the cash book but do not yet appear on the bank statement

Activity answers

Activity 1: Bank reconciliation – Bike Business

(a) to (c)

Cash book

Date 20XX	Details	Bank £	Date 20XX	Cheque number	Details	Bank £
01 Sept	Balance b/f	9,579	02 Sept	3456	QSH Ltd	2,960
21 Sept	PWG Ltd	6,850	08 Sept	3457	TGM Ltd	4,900
29 Sept	WTY Ltd	590	15 Sept	3458	FTJ Ltd	1,000
13 Sept	**Bank interest**	**60**	18 Sept	DD	Elec Ltd	650
29 Sept	**ESD Ltd**	**450**	24 Sept	3459	YHL Ltd	2,700
			30 Sept	3460	WMB Ltd	760
			25 Sept		**Bank charges**	**50**
			25 Sept	**DD**	**FRD Ltd**	**297**
			30 Sept		**Balance c/d**	**4,212**
		17,529				17,529
1 Oct	**Balance b/d**	**4,212**				

(d)

Bank reconciliation statement	£
Balance per bank statement	4,382
Add:	
WTY Ltd	590
Total to add	590
Less:	
WMB Ltd	760
Total to subtract	760
Balance as per cash book	4,212

Tutorial note

Difference in opening balances

The balance b/f on the bank statement at 1 September is £10,879.

The balance b/f on the cash book is £9,579.

Difference of £1,300 (due to cheque 3449 which would have been included in last month's bank reconciliation statement).

Having compared the cash book with the bank statement and ticked the items that are already included in both documents, we can see there are several items that need to be added to the cash book or included on the bank reconciliation statement.

Cash book

The paid-in side of the bank statement shows bank interest of £60 and a receipt from ESD Ltd of £450. These items are not yet included in the cash book and therefore must be recorded on the debit side, as they are an increase to the cash book balance.

Similarly, the paid-out side of the bank statement shows bank charges of £50 and a direct debit payment to FRD Ltd of £297. These items are not yet included in the cash book and therefore must be recorded on the credit side, as they are a decrease to the cash book balance.

Bank statement

The receipt from WTY Ltd of £590 is on the debit side of the cash book. When it clears the bank statement it will increase the balance. Therefore, it is included under the Add heading.

The payment to WMB Ltd of £760 is on the credit side of the cash book. Therefore, when it clears the bank statement it will decrease the bank balance. For this reason, it is included under the Less heading.

Activity 2: Updating the cash book

Cash book

Date 20XX	Details	Bank £	Date 20XX	Cheque number	Details	Bank £
01 Nov	Balance b/f	7,660	01 Nov	7823	RFT Ltd	980
18 Nov	MPV Ltd	2,780	02 Nov	7824	JGB Ltd	4,654
28 Nov	NON Ltd	420	15 Nov	7825	DER Ltd	650
28 Nov	**WD Ltd**	**476**	20 Nov	7826	WTR Ltd	410
			25 Nov	DD	SAO Ltd	730
			28 Nov	7827	REW Ltd	147
			30 Nov	7828	YLK Ltd	589
			10 Nov		**Bank interest**	**125**
			24 Nov	**SO**	**A Motor Co**	**500**
			30 Nov		**Bank charges**	**75**
			30 Nov		**Balance c/d**	**2,476**
		11,336				**11,336**
1 Dec	**Balance b/d**	**2,476**				

Tutorial note

Difference in opening balances

The balance b/f 2 November on the bank statement is £7,890.

The balance b/f in the cash book is £7,660.

Difference of £230 (due to cheque 7818 which would have been included in last month's bank reconciliation statement).

Cash book

The paid-in side of the bank statement includes a receipt from WD Ltd of £476. This item is not yet included in the cash book and therefore must be recorded on the debit side, as it increases the cash book balance.

The paid-out side of the bank statement contains several items that reduce the bank balance and need to be entered on the credit side of the cash book. The items are bank interest (£125), A Motor Co (£500) and bank charges (£75).

Activity 3: Bank reconciliation statement

(a)

Bank reconciliation statement	£
Balance per bank statement	1,631
Add:	
Beaker plc	3,245
Gilchrist Ltd	2,416
Total to add	5,661
Less:	
Tonks & Co	1,020
Taylor Agencies	547
Total to subtract	1,567
Balance as per cash book	5,725

Tutorial note

Difference in opening balances

The balance b/f in the cash book is £635.

The balance b/f on the bank statement is £385.

Difference of £250 (due to cheque 007303 which would have been included in last month's bank reconciliation statement).

Bank reconciliation

Having compared the cash book with the bank statement and ticked the items that are included in both documents, we can see that there are four items in the cash book but missing from the bank statement.

The receipts from Beaker plc of £3,245 and Gilchrist Ltd of £2,416 are on the debit side of the cash book but not shown on the bank statement. This means that when they clear, the bank statement will show an increase in the bank balance. Therefore, they are included under the Add heading of the reconciliation statement.

The payments to Tonks & Co of £1,020 and Taylor Agencies of £547 are on the credit side of the cash book. Therefore, when they clear, the bank statement will show a decrease the bank balance. For this reason, they are included under the Less heading.

(b)

Balance carried down £	Bank column totals £
5,725	12,164

Tutorial note

The debit side of the cash book is the higher of the two sides, and gives a bank column total of £12,164. When adding up the transactions on the credit side of the cash book, the amount is initially £6,439. By inserting a balance carried down of £5,725 (£12,164 minus £6,439), the debit side bank column total equals the credit side bank total column, and the cash book balances.

This also proves the reconciliation is correct as the balance c/d per the cash book is the same as the balance calculated through the reconciliation statement.

Cash book

Date 20XX	Details	Bank £	Date 20XX	Cheque number	Details	Bank £
15 June	PKL Ltd	4,000	01 June		Balance b/f	635
20 June	Beaker plc	3,245	01 June	07315	Abby Photos	483
21 June	Bissell & Co	2,500	06 June	07316	LTL Ltd	2,165
22 June	Gilchrist Ltd	2,416	06 June	07317	Retro Frames	1,233
22 June	Bank interest	3	22 June	07318	Tonks & Co	1,020
			22 June	07319	Taylor Agencies	547
			20 June	DD	Hampton CC	135
			20 June	DD	Motor Mania	177
			22 June		Bank charges	44
			22 June		**Balance c/d**	**5,725**
		12,164				**12,164**

Test your learning

1 **If money is paid into a newly opened bank current account this will appear on the bank statement as (tick the appropriate option):**

A debit entry	
A credit entry	✓

2 **If a figure for bank interest appeared in the paid in column of the bank statement, this would be adjusted for in the (tick the appropriate option):**

Debit side of the cash book	✓
Credit side of the cash book	

3 **A standing order payment is on the bank statement but has been omitted from the cash book. This should be adjusted for in the (tick the appropriate option):**

Debit side of the cash book	
Credit side of the cash book	✓

Paid out Dr Bank Stat.
Paid in CR -"-
operation on cash book opposite side

4 **A cheque in the credit side of the cash book is unticked after the bank statement and cash book have been compared.**

How should this be dealt with in the bank reconciliation statement? (Tick the appropriate option):

As an unpresented cheque	✓
As an outstanding lodgement	

5   Bremner Ltd received the following bank statement for February.

Date 20XX	Details	Paid out £	Paid in £	Balance £	
03 Feb	Balance b/f			6,230 ✓	C
03 Feb	Cheque 003252	2,567 ✓		3,663	C
03 Feb	Cheque 003253	333 ✓		3,330	C
03 Feb	Cheque 003254	1,006 ✓		2,324	C
04 Feb	Cheque 003257	3,775 ✓		1,451	D
09 Feb	Branthill Co		1,559	108	C
11 Feb	Cheque 003255	966 ✓		858	D
13 Feb	DD AxDC	250 ✓		1,108	D
18 Feb	DD Trust Insurance	325		1,433	D
20 Feb	Bank charges	14		1,447	D
22 Feb	Interest charge	56		1,503	D
23 Feb	Counter credit	CR cash book	2,228 ✓	725	C
	D = Debit, C = Credit DR cash book				

The cash book as at 23 February is shown below.

(a) **Check the items on the bank statement against the items in the cash book.**

(b) **Using the picklist below for the details column, enter any items in the cash book as needed.**

(c) **Total the cash book and clearly show the balance carried down at 23 February and brought down at 24 February.**

(d) **Identify the four transactions that are included in the cash book but missing from the bank statement, and complete the bank reconciliation statement as at 23 February using the picklist.**

Cash book

Date 20XX	Details	Bank £	Date 20XX	Cheque number	Details	Bank £
01 Feb	Balance b/f	6,230	01 Feb	003252	Jeggers Ltd	2,567
20 Feb	Straightens Co	2,228	01 Feb	003253	Short & Fell	333
21 Feb	Plumpers	925	01 Feb	003254	Rastop Ltd	1,006
22 Feb	Eastern Supplies	1,743	01 Feb	003255	A & D Trading	966
		1559	02 Feb	003256	Jesmond Warr	2,309
			02 Feb	003257	Nistral Ltd	3,775
			13 Feb	003258	Simpsons	449
			13 Feb		AxDC	250
						3e5
						14
						56
					c/d	635
		12685				12685
	b/d	635				

Bank reconciliation statement	£
Balance per bank statement	725
Add:	
925 +1743	2668
Total to add	
Less:	
2309 + 449	2758
Total to subtract	
Balance as per cash book	635

Picklist:

A & D Trading
AxDC
Balance b/d
Balance c/d
Bank charges
Branthill Co
Closing balance
Eastern Supplies
Interest charge
Jeggers Ltd
Jesmond Warr
Nistral Ltd
Opening balance
Plumpers
Rastop Ltd
Short & Fell
Simpsons
Straightens Co
Trust Insurance

Introduction to control accounts

Learning outcomes

Having studied this chapter, you will be able to:

2.1	**Identify the purpose of control accounts**
	• The purpose of the sales and purchases ledger control accounts (part of the double-entry bookkeeping system)
	• The purpose of the VAT control account
2.2	**Identify the purpose of reconciliation**
	• Reasons for reconciling the sales and purchases ledger control accounts with the sales and purchases ledgers
3.1	**Produce control accounts**
	• Prepare control accounts: sales ledger, purchases ledger, VAT
	• Total and balance control accounts:
	– balance carried down
	– balance brought down

Assessment context

Control accounts are a key part of the syllabus. You need to understand the purpose of the sales, purchases and VAT control account and the reasons why the sales ledger control account is reconciled with the sales ledger, and the purchases ledger control account reconciled with the purchases ledger. This sets the scene for the questions we will see in the next chapter and could be tested in a knowledge-based task. The VAT control account is another general ledger account and one which you should learn how to prepare.

Qualification context

In the *Advanced bookkeeping* unit you could be required to identify the reasons why reconciliations are carried out, as well as to determine the adjustments that may need to be made, to the control account balance and/or the individual sales or purchases ledger balance.

Business context

Businesses must be able to account for their customers and suppliers efficiently and accurately. This enables them to chase up overdue balances from credit customers and ensure that their suppliers are paid on a timely basis. They must also identify VAT transactions and make appropriate payments to HMRC.

Chapter overview

- SLCA: the total owed by all credit customers at a particular point in time
- PLCA: the total owed to all credit suppliers at a particular point in time

- SL: a list of the amounts owed by each individual credit customer at a particular point in time
- PL: a list of the amounts owed to each individual credit supplier at a particular point in time

Reconciliations

**Sales ledger control account
Purchases ledger control account**

**Sales ledger
Purchases ledger**

Introduction to control accounts

VAT control account

- VAT control account is used to calculate the net amount due to the tax authorities

Introduction

In earlier studies we have seen that business transactions are recorded in the books of prime entry. In particular:

- Sales invoices sent to credit customers are recorded in the sales day book

- Purchases invoices received from credit suppliers are recorded in the purchases day book

- Cash received from customers or paid to suppliers is noted in the cash book

- Credit notes received from credit customers are recorded in the sales returns day book

- Credit notes sent to credit suppliers are recorded in the purchases returns day book

- Prompt payments discounts taken by credit customers are recorded in the discounts allowed day book

- Prompt payments discounts given by credit suppliers are recorded in the discounts received day book

Having been recorded in the day books, these transactions will then be included in the relevant ledgers. All day books are totalled periodically and the totals are posted to the relevant control account (which forms part of the double entry bookkeeping system). Individual items are posted to the ledger accounts (which sit outside the main ledger).

Three important control accounts are:

- Sales ledger control account – which shows the amount owed by credit customers

- Purchases ledger control account – which shows the amount owed to credit suppliers

- VAT control account – which shows the amount due or reclaimable from HMRC

The sales ledger control account is supported by the sales ledger and the purchases ledger control account is supported by the purchases ledger.

1 Recap from earlier studies

1.1 Recording credit sales and purchases in the general ledger (recap)

From your previous accounting studies you are familiar with the concept that credit sales and purchases (and any returns that arise) are entered in the main ledger with the following journals:

(a) **Main ledger – total credit sales for a particular period**

Account name	Debit √	Credit √
Sales ledger control	√	
VAT		√
Sales		√

(b) **Main ledger – total credit sales returns for a particular period**

Account name	Debit √	Credit √
Sales returns	√	
VAT	√	
Sales ledger control		√

(c) **Main ledger – total purchases for a particular period**

Account name	Debit √	Credit √
Purchases	√	
VAT	√	
Purchases ledger control		√

(d) **Main ledger – total purchases returns for a particular period**

Account name	Debit √	Credit √
Purchases ledger control	√	
VAT		√
Purchases returns		√

Activity 1: Double entry (credit sales)

In the month of January, a VAT registered business makes sales on credit of £20,000 excluding VAT.

What is the double entry to this in the general ledger?

Account name	Amount £	Debit √	Credit √
SALES LEDGER CONTROL	24,000	√	
VAT	4,000		√
SALES	20,000		√

Picklist:

Bank
Purchases
Purchases ledger control
Purchases returns
Sales
Sales ledger control
Sales returns
VAT

Activity 2: Double entry (credit purchases)

In the month of January, a VAT registered business makes purchases on credit of £10,000 excluding VAT.

What is the double entry to this in the general ledger?

Account name	Amount £	Debit √	Credit √
PURCHASE LEDGER CONTROL	12,000		√
VAT	2,000	√	
PURCHASES	10,000	√	

Picklist:

Bank
Purchases
Purchases ledger control
Purchases returns
Sales
Sales ledger control
Sales returns
VAT

1.2 Prompt payment discounts (recap)

When a credit customer takes advantage of a prompt payment discount, this must be recorded in the ledgers. The entries are as follows.

Discounts allowed

Main ledger – discounts allowed

Account name	Debit √	Credit √
Discounts allowed	√	
VAT	√	
Sales ledger control		√

The credit entry to the sales ledger control account balance is for the gross amount as the full amount settled by way of the discount is no longer owed by the customer. The VAT element is posted to the VAT account cancelling out the VAT which arose on the original sale. The net amount is posted as a debit to the discounts allowed account, being an increase in expenses.

Sales ledger – discounts allowed

Account name	Debit √	Credit √
Customer X		√

The sales ledger is credited with the full amount (gross amount) settled by way of the discount as this is no longer owed by the customer.

Discounts received

Main ledger – discounts received

Account name	Debit √	Credit √
Purchases ledger control	√	
VAT		√
Discounts received		√

The debit entry to the purchases ledger control account is for the gross amount as the full amount settled by way of the discount is no longer owed to the supplier. The VAT element is posted to the VAT account cancelling out the VAT which arose on the original purchase. The net amount is posted as a credit to the discounts received account, being an increase in income.

Purchases ledger – discounts received

Account name	Debit √	Credit √
Supplier Y	√	

The purchases ledger is debited with the full amount settled by way of the discount as this is no longer owed to the supplier.

2 Control accounts

2.1 Purpose of control accounts

Control accounts contain summarised totals of all the individual transactions affecting their respective ledgers. They contain the same information as is in the sales and purchases accounts in the ledgers; however, they show the totals rather than the individual transactions.

Control accounts are mainly used for trade receivables (credit customers), trade payables (credit suppliers) and VAT.

The sales ledger control account is an account in which records are kept of transactions involving all credit customers in total.

A purchases ledger control account is an account in which records are kept of transactions involving all credit suppliers in total.

The control account system therefore means that:

- Transactions posted to the general ledger are kept to a minimum so there is less room for error in the general ledger double entry system

- It is easy at any point in time to identify from the general ledger how much in total the business owes and is owed

- The accuracy of the general ledger and the subsidiary ledgers can be checked by reconciling the balance on the control account in the former, to the total of the balances on the latter. This prompts the business to identify and deal with discrepancies quickly

- Segregation of duties is promoted within the organisation as one person could maintain the sales and purchases ledger accounts and another person could maintain the control accounts. This reduces the risk of fraud

Also, and as you have seen when preparing an initial trial balance in earlier studies, control accounts are general ledger accounts which form part of the double entry bookkeeping system. Therefore, the year end balances are ultimately included in the final accounts.

2.2 Preparing control accounts

A typical sales ledger control account will be structured as follows:

Sales ledger control

Details	Amount £	Details	Amount £
Balance b/d	X	Bank	X
Credit sales	X	Sales returns	X
		Discounts allowed	X
		Balance c/d	X
	X		X
Balance b/d	X		

Explanation

Details	Explanation
Balance b/d	This is normally on the left hand side of the sales ledger control account. This is because the credit customers owe money to the business and therefore the balance b/d is an asset.
Balance c/d	This is a balancing figure which enables the totals on both sides of the T account to equal each other. It is usually a balancing figure on the right hand side of the T account.
Credit sales	Credit sales increase the amount owed by credit customers. Therefore, a debit entry is posted to the control account, reflecting the increase in the asset.
Bank	When credit customers are paid the amount owed there is a decrease in the sales ledger control account asset. Therefore, this entry is on the right hand side of the account.
Sales returns	Sales returns decrease the asset as the customers have returned the items they originally bought, and therefore no longer owe money to the business. Therefore, this entry is on the right hand side of the account.
Discounts allowed	If amounts owed by credit customers are partially settled through discounts allowed, this also reduces the sales ledger control account asset. Therefore, this entry is on the right hand side of the account.

A typical purchase ledger control account will be structured as follows:

Purchases ledger control

Details	Amount £	Details	Amount £
Bank	X	Balance b/d	X
Purchases returns	X	Credit purchases	X
Discounts received	X		
Balance c/d	X		
	X		X
		Balance b/d	X

Explanation

Details	Explanation
Balance b/d	This is normally on the right hand side of the purchases ledger control account. This is because the business owes money to the credit supplier and therefore the balance b/d is a liability.
Balance c/d	This is a balancing figure which enables the totals on both sides of the T account to equal each other. It is usually a balancing figure on the left hand side of the T account.
Credit purchases	Credit purchases increase the liability as the business owes suppliers for the items bought on credit. Therefore, this entry is to the credit side of the account.
Bank	When credit suppliers are paid the amount owed there is a decrease in the purchases ledger control account liability. Therefore, this entry is on the left hand side of the account.
Purchases returns	Purchases returns decrease the liability as the business has returned the items they originally bought, and therefore no longer owe money to the supplier. Therefore, this entry is on the left hand side of the account.
Discount received	If an amount owed to credit suppliers is partially settled through a discount, this reduces the purchases ledger control account liability. Therefore, this entry is also on the left hand side of the account.

3 Purpose of subsidiary ledger accounts

Subsidiary ledger accounts are prepared so that the business can see the amount owed from credit customers or to credit suppliers at a point in time. The sales ledger contains separate accounts for each credit customer and the purchases ledger contains separate accounts for each credit supplier. The separate accounts list all transactions (invoices, credit notes, payments etc) relating to individual credit customers/suppliers.

If the double entry in the general ledger and the entries in the subsidiary ledger have all been entered correctly, the total of the list of balances in the ledgers will always equal the balance on the respective control account.

Illustration 1: The accounting system for credit sales

We will see how the sales ledger and sales ledger control accounts are created and reconciled through an illustration.

W Johnson has two credit customers, A and B. On 1 May 20XX, Customer A owes £300 and Customer B owes £170 (therefore £470 in total).

In May the following transactions occur and are recorded in the day books.

The sales day book is used to record all invoices sent to customers buying on credit.

Sales day book (extract)

Date 20XX	Details	Invoice number	Total £	VAT £	Net £
3 May	A	0045	240	40	200
8 May	B	0046	180	30	150
20 May	B	0047	120	20	100
28 May	A	0049	216	36	180
	Totals		756	126	630

If items are returned by customers, credit notes are recorded in the sales returns day book.

Sales returns day book (extract)

Date 20XX	Details	Credit note number	Total £	VAT £	Net £
12 May	A	CN012	240	40	200
30 May	B	CN015	120	20	100
	Totals		360	60	300

Money received from credit customers is entered in the debit side of the cash book.

Cash book – debit side (extract)

Date 20XX	Details	Bank £	Trade receivables £
21 May	A	276	276
25 May	B	170	170
	Totals	446	446

Where the customer decides to take a prompt payment discount, the business issues a credit note which is recorded in the discounts allowed day book.

Discounts allowed day book (extract)

Details	Total £	VAT £	Net £
Customer A	24	4	20
Totals	24	4	20

Having recorded the transactions in the day books, the business then needs to understand:

- The amount owed by customers A and B at the end of the month
- The effect these transactions have on the general ledger

Sales ledger

The subsidiary sales ledger for W Johnson in May will be as follows:

Customer A – Sales ledger account

Details	Amount £	Details	Amount £
Balance b/d	300	Credit note	240
Invoice	240	Bank	276
Invoice	216	Discounts allowed	24
		Balance c/d	216
	756		756
Balance b/d	216		

Customer B – Sales ledger account

Details	Amount £	Details	Amount £
Balance b/d	170	Credit note	120
Invoice	180	Bank	170
Invoice	120	Balance c/d	180
	470		470
Balance b/d	180		

Therefore, it can be seen that the sales ledger accounts show the amount owed by each individual customer at a point in time.

Sales ledger control account

The sales ledger control account for W Johnson in May will be as follows:

Sales ledger control account

Details	Amount £	Details	Amount £
Balance b/d	470	Sales returns	360
Sales	756	Bank	446
		Discounts allowed	24
		Balance c/d	396
	1,226		1,226
Balance b/d	396		

In this illustration for W Johnson, it can be seen that the closing balance b/d in the sales ledger control account at the end of the month equals the total of the individual balances on the sales ledgers accounts for customers A and B.

Reconciliation

Details	Amount £
Customer A	216
Customer B	180
Total of the sales ledger account balances	396
Balance b/d at the end of May in the sales ledger control account	396
Difference	nil

This suggests that the transactions have been correctly recorded in the accounting records.

4 Diagram – accounting system for credit sales

This whole process of accounting for credit sales in the general ledger and in the sales ledger, ignoring credit notes and discounts for now, can be illustrated in a diagram:

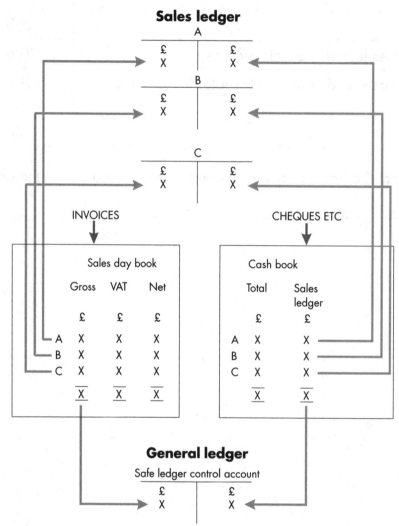

🎨 Illustration 2: The accounting system for credit purchases

In this next illustration we will see how the subsidiary purchases ledger and purchases ledger control account are created and reconciled.

W Johnson purchases goods on credit from suppliers C and D. On 1 May 20XX, W Johnson owes supplier C £250 and owes supplier D £140 (therefore £390 in total).

In May the following transactions occur and are recorded in the day books.

The purchases day book is used to record all invoices received from suppliers when purchasing on credit.

Purchases day book (extract)

Date 20XX	Details	Invoice number	Total £	VAT £	Net £
5 May	C	CC10	96	16	80
10 May	C	CC18	144	24	120
15 May	D	LV73	90	15	75
27 May	D	LV80	252	42	210
	Totals		582	97	485

If items are returned to suppliers, credit notes are recorded in the purchases returns day book.

Purchases returns day book (extract)

Date 20XX	Details	Credit note number	Total £	VAT £	Net £
12 May	C	CN33	96	16	80
30 May	D	CN104	252	42	210
	Totals		348	58	290

Money paid to credit suppliers is entered in the credit side of the cash book.

Cash book – credit side (extract)

Date 20XX	Details	Bank £	Trade payables £
21 May	C	250	250
25 May	D	128	128
	Totals	378	378

Where the business decides to take a prompt payment discount, the credit note detailing this transaction is recorded in the discounts received day book.

Discounts received day book (extract)

Details	Total £	VAT £	Net £
Supplier D	12	2	10
Totals	12	2	10

Purchases ledger

The subsidiary purchases ledger for W Johnson in May will be as follows:

Supplier C – Purchases ledger account

Details	Amount £	Details	Amount £
Credit note	96	Balance b/d	250
Bank	250	Invoice	96
Balance c/d	144	Invoice	144
	490		490
		Balance b/d	144

Suppliers D – Purchases ledger account

Details	Amount £	Details	Amount £
Credit note	252	Balance b/d	140
Bank	128	Invoice	90
Discount received	12	Invoice	252
Balance c/d	90		
	482		482
		Balance b/d	90

The purchases ledger control account for W Johnson in May will be as follows:

Purchases ledger control

Details	Amount £	Details	Amount £
Purchase returns	348	Balance b/d	390
Bank	378	Credit purchases	582
Discounts received	12		
Balance c/d	234		
	972		972
		Balance b/d	234

In this illustration for W Johnson, it can be seen that the closing balance b/d in the purchases ledger control account at the end of the month equals the total of the individual balances on the purchases ledger accounts for suppliers C and D.

Reconciliation

Details	Amount £
Supplier C	144
Supplier D	90
Total of the subsidiary purchase ledger account balances	234
Balance b/d at the end of May in the purchase ledger control account	234
Difference	nil

This suggests that the transactions have been correctly recorded in the accounting records.

Regular reconciliations between the control account and ledger helps to ensure that the accounting records are accurate as discrepancies can quickly be identified and corrected.

However, note that it does not prevent all errors from occurring. For example, if a purchases invoice was accidently omitted from the purchases day book, this would not be identified by a reconciliation as both the purchases ledger and purchases ledger control account would be understated in respect of this transaction.

5 Diagram – accounting system for credit purchases

This whole process of accounting for credit purchases in the general ledger and in the purchases ledger, ignoring credit notes and discounts, can be illustrated in a diagram:

6 VAT control account

6.1 Recap of VAT

A further control account to consider is the VAT control account. Before we look at this account, it is useful to recap the principles of VAT seen in your earlier studies.

In the UK VAT is administered and regulated by Her Majesty's Revenue and Customs (HMRC). VAT is a tax on consumers that is collected on behalf of HMRC by VAT registered businesses.

Not all businesses are registered for VAT. This means they cannot charge VAT on their sales or reclaim it on their purchases.

Those that are must (generally) charge 20% VAT on top of their sales and can reclaim VAT on their purchases.

Illustration 3: VAT transactions

Example of VAT on sales

Net sales price	£100.00	Revenue retained by the business
VAT @ 20%	£ 20.00	**Owed to HMRC**
Gross sales price	£120.00	Received from customer

In this illustration, the business retains £100.00 and records this as its sales revenue. When the VAT payment is due, it must hand over £20.00 to HMRC. It is, therefore, the customer who will have paid the VAT.

VAT charged on the sales price is referred to as **output tax.**

Example of VAT on purchases

Net purchase price	£40.00	Expense actually suffered by the business
VAT @ 20%	£ 8.00	**VAT a registered business can claim back**
Gross purchase price	£48.00	Amount paid to supplier

In this illustration, the business has to pay £48.00 but only suffers £40.00 as the VAT will be claimed back from HMRC.

VAT charged on the purchase price is referred to as **input tax.**

Payments to HMRC

At the end of the VAT period, the business will usually pay over to HMRC the excess of output tax over the input tax. In this illustration, the business would pay £12.00 to HMRC, being £20.00 output tax less £8.00 input tax.

If the business had paid more VAT to suppliers than it collected from customers, it would receive a refund from HMRC of the excess VAT paid.

6.2 Accounting for VAT

Output and input tax is accounted for at the same time as we record sales and purchases, but we must also account for payments of VAT owed to HMRC and refunds of VAT from them:

- The VAT amounts on sales and purchase invoices and credit notes, and on cash sales and purchases, are recorded in the day books and then totals are posted to the VAT control account.

- Payments to HMRC in respect of VAT owed are credited to the cash book and debited to the VAT control account.

- Receipts of VAT refunds from HMRC are debited to the cash book and credited to the VAT control account.

- The balance b/d on the VAT control account is the amount owed to (credit balance) or refundable by (debit balance) HMRC.

VAT control account

At the end of the VAT period the input tax is deducted from the output tax and the balance is paid to HMRC. The **VAT control account** is used to establish any balance due or reclaimable)

It is important to familiarise yourself with this account.

Illustration 4: Preparing the VAT control account

A business has a credit balance b/d on 1 November 20XX of £3,000.

During November the following information regarding VAT is recorded:

Details	Amount £
VAT on sales	5,000
VAT on sales returns	500
VAT on cash sales	300
VAT on purchases	4,000
VAT on purchase returns	600
VAT on discounts allowed	200
VAT on discounts received	100
Bank payment to HMRC	2,800

Prepare the VAT control account for November. Show the balance c/d at the end of the month and the balance b/d at the start of the next month.

VAT control account

Details	Amount £	Details	Amount £
Sales returns	500	Balance b/d	3,000
Purchases	4,000	Sales	5,000
Discounts allowed	200	Cash sales	300
Bank	2,800	Purchase returns	600
Balance c/d	1,500	Discounts received	100
	9,000		9,000
		Balance b/d	1,500

Explanation

Details	Explanation
Balance b/d	This is normally on the right hand side of the VAT control account as it is a **liability**. Why? Well, in any profitable business the sale price exceeds the purchase price. Therefore, VAT is owed to HMRC at the end of the VAT period (eg month/quarter).
Balance c/d	This is a **balancing figure** which enables the totals on both sides of the T account to equal each other. It is usually a balancing figure on the left hand side of the T account.
Sales	When a business makes a sale it must pay the VAT collected on behalf of the customer to HMRC. Therefore, a sale represents an **increase in liability**.
Cash sales	This works in the same way as credit sales, only the amounts involved will be smaller. There is still an **increase in liability** when a cash sale is made.
Purchases	When a business makes a purchase it can reclaim the VAT paid on that purchase from HMRC. Therefore, a purchase represents a **decrease in liability.**
Sales returns	This has the opposite effect of a sale and is a **decrease in liability.** The VAT liability goes down as the product is returned. Therefore, the VAT no longer needs to be paid to HMRC.
Purchase returns	This has the opposite effect of a purchase and is an **increase in liability.** The amount of VAT reclaimable has gone down as the business is returning the goods. Therefore, the VAT cannot be reclaimed from HMRC.
Discounts allowed	If a credit customer takes advantage of a prompt payment discount they owe less money to the business than is shown on the original sales invoice. Therefore the VAT due to HMRC decreases and so is entered as a debit on the VAT control account.
Discounts received	If a business pays promptly and takes advantage of a prompt payment discount they will pay less money to the supplier than is shown on the original purchase invoice. Therefore, the VAT reclaimable from HMRC decreases and so is entered as a credit on the VAT control account.
Bank	This is the payment made to HMRC or money received from them.

Activity 3: VAT control account

The following is an extract from Michael's books of prime entry.

Totals for quarter			
	£		£
Sales day book		**Purchases day book**	
Net:	220,000	Net:	140,000
VAT:	44,000	VAT:	28,000
Gross:	264,000	Gross:	168,000
Sales returns day book		**Purchases returns day book**	
Net:	35,920	Net:	24,040
VAT:	7,184	VAT:	4,808
Gross:	43,104	Gross:	28,848
Discounts allowed day book		**Discounts received day book**	
Discount allowed:	2,400	Discount received:	1,200
VAT:	480	VAT:	240
Total:	2,880	Total:	1,440
Cash book			
Net cash sales:	54,000		
VAT:	10,800		
Gross cash sales:	64,800		

(a) What will be the entries in the VAT control account to record the VAT transactions in the quarter?

35664

Account name	Amount £	Debit √	Credit √
Sales	44000		√
Purchases	28000	√	
Sales returns	7184	√	
Purchase returns	4808		√
Discount allowed	480	√	
Discount received	240		√
Cash book	10800		√

Picklist:

Bank
Cash sales
Discounts allowed
Discounts received
Purchases
Purchase returns
Sales
Sales returns
VAT

53 848   59 848
b/d 24 184

c/d
24184

input (related to purchases)

output TAX (related to sales)

The VAT return has been completed and shows an amount owing from HM Revenue and Customs of £24,184.

(b) Answer the following question.

Question	Yes √	No √
Is the VAT return correct?	√	√

Chapter summary

- The subsidiary sales ledger and purchases ledger and the sales and purchases control accounts are both prepared from information included in the books of prime entry.

- However, the subsidiary sales ledger and purchases ledger sit outside the general ledger. They enable businesses to see the amount owed by individual credit customers and the amount owed to credit suppliers.

- The sales and purchases ledger control accounts sit within the general ledger. They enable the business to see the total amount owed by credit customers and owed to credit suppliers.

- Reconciliations between the sales ledger and the sales ledger control account and the purchases ledger and purchases ledger control account are important and help to ensure the accounting records are free from error.

- The VAT control account is used for all transactions related to VAT, and allows the business to identify clearly how much is owed to HMRC in respect of VAT in a period, or how much is due from them.

Keywords

- **Control account:** A general ledger account that includes totals from the books of prime entry. This helps ensure that postings to the general ledger are complete and accurate

- **Purchases ledger:** Contains separate accounts for each credit supplier so that at any time, a business knows how much it owes to each supplier

- **Purchases ledger control account:** Totals for all the credit purchases transactions are posted to this account

- **Sales ledger:** Contains separate accounts for each credit customer so that, at any time, a business knows how much it is owed by each customer

- **Sales ledger control account:** Totals for all the credit sales transactions are posted to this account

- **Subsidiary ledgers:** The sales ledger and purchase ledgers, which contain a ledger account for each individual credit customer or credit supplier. They are not part of the general ledger

- **VAT control account:** Used for all transactions related to VAT, and allows the business to identify clearly how much is owed to HM Revenue & Customs in respect of VAT in a period, or how much is due from them

Activity answers

Activity 1: Double entry (credit sales)

Account name	Amount £	Debit √	Credit √
Sales ledger control	24,000	√	
VAT	4,000		√
Sales	20,000		√

The sales ledger control account is debited with the gross amount as the customer owes the full amount (VAT and net). The debit entry relates to the increase in asset.

A credit is made to the VAT account, as this is an increase in the amount owed to the tax authorities, and therefore the liability rises. A credit is also made to the sales account for the net amount, being the increase in income.

Activity 2: Double entry (credit purchases)

Account name	Amount £	Debit √	Credit √
Purchases	10,000	√	
VAT	2,000	√	
Purchases ledger control	12,000		√

A debit is made to purchases as this is an increase in expenses. The net amount is recorded in this account. A debit is also made to the VAT account as the money is reclaimable from the tax authorities, and therefore this is a reduction in the VAT liability.

A credit is made to the purchases ledger control account as this is a liability (the gross amount will be paid to the supplier).

Activity 3: VAT control account

(a) What will be the entries in the VAT control account to record the VAT transactions in the quarter?

Account name	Amount £	Debit √	Credit √
Sales	44,000		√
Sales returns	7,184	√	
Purchases	28,000	√	
Purchases returns	4,808		√
Discounts allowed	480	√	
Discounts received	240		√
Cash sales	10,800		√

The VAT relating to sales (both credit and cash sales) are included on the credit side of the VAT control account as this money is owed to the tax authorities.

The VAT on purchases is recorded on the debit side of the VAT control account as this money is reclaimable from the tax authorities. The debit is effectively a reduction in the liability.

The VAT on returns is included on the opposite side to the VAT recorded when the original transactions occurred, thereby cancelling out the VAT which arose on those sales or purchases.

(b) Answer the following question.

Question	Yes √	No √
Is the VAT return correct?		√

If the VAT control account is balanced off it shows a liability **due to** HMRC of £24,184. It is not due from HMRC.

Test your learning

1   In the month of March, a VAT registered business receives sales returns of £1,800 from credit customers including VAT.

What is the double entry to record this in the general ledger? Ignore VAT.

Account name	Amount £	Debit √	Credit √
Sales returns	1500 (300)	√	
SLCA	1800		√
VAT	300	√	

Picklist:

Bank
Purchases
Purchases ledger control
Purchases returns
Sales
Sales ledger control
Sales returns
VAT

2   In the month of April, a VAT registered business returns goods it had purchased on credit costing £900 including VAT.

What is the double entry to record this in the general ledger? Ignore VAT.

Account name	Amount £	Debit √	Credit √
PLCA	900	√	
Purchase returns	750 (150)		√
VAT	150		√

Picklist:

Bank
Purchases
Purchases ledger control
Purchases returns
Sales
Sales ledger control
Sales returns
VAT

3 DP is a small VAT registered company that currently has only two credit customers. The opening balances on the sales ledger accounts at the start of May 20XX were as follows:

SLCA

	£
Virgo Partners	227.58
McGowan & Sons	552.73

The opening balance on the sales ledger control account at the start of May was £780.31. ✓

The sales day book and cash book – debit side for May are given below:

Sales day book

Date	Customer	Total £	VAT £	Net £
10 May	Virgo Partners	96.72	16.12	80.60
20 May	McGowan & Sons	595.08	99.18	495.90
30 May	Virgo Partners	214.44	35.74	178.70
		906.24 ✓	151.04	755.20

Cash book – debit side

Date	Details	Bank £	Trade receivables £
4 May	Virgo Partners	117.38	117.38
15 May	McGowan & Sons	552.73	552.73
		670.11	670.11

(a) **Write up the sales ledger control account for the month and the individual sales ledger accounts.**

(b) **Agree the control account balance to the total of the subsidiary sales ledger account balances at the end of the month.**

Reconciliation

	Amount £
Sales ledger control account balance as at 31 May	1016.44
Total of sales ledger accounts as at 31 May *(add up both customers)*	1016.44
Difference	—

4   DP is a small VAT registered business with two credit suppliers. The opening balances on its purchases ledger accounts at the start of May were:

	£
Jenkins Suppliers	441.56
Kilnfarm Paper	150.00

The opening balance on the purchases ledger control account at the start of May was £591.56

The purchases day book and cash book – credit side for the period are given below:

Purchases day book

Date	Supplier	Total £	VAT £	Net £
5 May	Kilnfarm Paper	153.12	25.52	127.60
10 May	Jenkins Suppliers	219.96	36.66	183.30
20 May	Kilnfarm Paper	153.12	25.52	127.60
27 May	Jenkins Suppliers	451.32	75.22	376.10
		977.52	162.92	814.60

Cash book – credit side

Date	Details	Bank £	Trade payables £
10 May	Jenkins Suppliers	441.56	441.56
12 May	Kilnfarm Paper	150.00	150.00
27 May	Kilnfarm Paper	153.12	153.12
		744.68	744.68

(a) **Write up the purchases ledger control account for May and the individual purchases ledger accounts.**

(b) **Agree the control account balance at the end of May to the total of the list of individual balances in the subsidiary purchases ledger.**

General ledger

Purchases ledger control

Details	Amount £	Details	Amount £
Bank	744.68	b/d	591.56
c/d	824.4	Purchases	977.52
	1569.08		1569.08
		b/d	824.4

Picklist:

Balance b/d
Balance c/d
Bank
Purchases

Purchases ledger

Jenkins Suppliers

Details	Amount £	Details	Amount £
Bank	441.56	B/d	441.56
		INV 10 May	219.96
c/d	671.28	INV 27 May	451.32
	1112.84		1112.84
		b/d	671.28

Kilnfarm Paper

Details	Amount £	Details	Amount £
Bank	303.12	B/d	150
		INV 5 May	153.12
old)	153.12	INV 20 May	153.12
	456.24		456.24
		b/d	153.12

Picklist:

Balance b/d
Balance c/d
Bank
Invoice

Reconciliation

	£
Purchases ledger control account balance as at 31 May	824.40
Total of purchases ledger accounts as at 31 May	824.40
Difference	—

5   The following is an extract from a business's books of prime entry.

Totals for three month period			
Sales day book		**Purchases day book**	
Net:	£145,360	Net:	£71,840
VAT:	£29,072	VAT:	£14,368
Total:	£174,432	Total:	£86,208
Sales returns day book		**Purchases returns day book**	
Net:	£4,290	Net:	£2,440
VAT:	£858	VAT:	£488
Total:	£5,148	Total:	£2,928
Cash book			
Net cash sales:	£1,660		
VAT:	£332		
Total cash sales:	£1,992		

(a) **Using the picklist to complete the details columns, make the required entries in the VAT control account to record the VAT transactions in the period.**

15226 **VAT control** 29892

Details	Amount £	Details	Amount £
Purchases	14,368	Sales	29,072
Sales ret.	858	Purchase ret.	488
	c/d 14 666	Cash book	332

29892

Picklist:

Cash sales
Purchases
Purchases returns
Sales
Sales returns

balance
DR > CR owing

29892
b/d 14666
INPUT

The VAT return has been completed and shows an amount owing from HM Revenue & Customs of £14,666.

(b) **Is the VAT return correct?**

	✓
Yes	
No	✓

Preparing and reconciling control accounts

Learning outcomes

Having studied this chapter you will be able to:

3.1	**Produce control accounts**
	• Prepare control accounts:
	– Sales ledger
	– Purchases ledger
	• Total and balance control accounts:
	– Balance carried down
	– Balance brought down
3.2	**Reconcile control accounts**
	• Total the balances of the individual sales and purchases ledger accounts:
	– Sales ledger debit/credit balances
	– Purchases ledger debit/credit balances
	• Identify discrepancies between the sales and purchases ledger control accounts and the individual ledgers
	• Identify reasons for discrepancies between the sales and purchases ledger control accounts and the individual ledgers
2.3	**Identify the purpose of the journal**
	• Transactions that are recorded in the journal:
	– Irrecoverable debts written off
4.1	**Produce journal entries to record accounting transactions**
	• Identify and record entries to write off irrecoverable debts:
	– Record VAT
	– Where appropriate, calculate VAT from gross and net amounts

Assessment context

Control accounts are a key part of the syllabus and an important part of the assessment. You will be asked to prepare the sales or purchase ledger control account and reconcile the control account with the relevant ledger account.

You may be asked to prepare control accounts in T account format. Alternatively, you may have to present your answer in tabular format, by selecting an account name from a picklist, entering the correct amount, and then using tick marks to indicate debit and credit entries.

Qualification context

In the *Advanced bookkeeping* unit you could be required to identify the reasons why reconciliations are carried out as well as to determine the adjustments that may need to be made either to the control account balance and/or the individual sales or purchase ledger balance.

Business context

Businesses need to know the amount owed by their customers and to their suppliers at any given point in time. This encourages strong business relationships and efficient cash management.

Chapter overview

The SLCA and the SL and the PLCA and the PL are showing information from the same source (totals and individual accounts) so the overall balance should reconcile.

Reconciliations

- SLCA: the total owed by all credit customers at a particular point in time
- PLCA: the total owed to all credit suppliers at a particular point in time

- SL: a list of the amounts owed by each individual credit customer at a particular point in time
- PL: a list of the amounts owed to each individual credit supplier at a particular point in time

**Sales ledger control account
Purchases ledger control account**

**Sales ledger
Purchases ledger**

Using control accounts

Credit control

- Credit control is the process of ensuring credit customers pay on a timely basis
- An aged receivables analysis enables the business to see the total amount owed by each customer and the age of the invoices

Irrecoverable debts

- If a credit customer cannot pay, the amount must be written off as an irrecoverable debt
- The journal to record an irrecoverable debt write-off is:

  Dr irrecoverable debt expense

  Dr VAT

  Cr sales ledger control

Introduction

As we saw in the previous chapter, it is important to prepare sales and purchases control accounts. This enables the business to see the total amount due from credit customers and the total owed to credit suppliers at any point in time.

Individual sales and purchase ledgers are also maintained so that the business can see the amount owed by specific customers and due to specific suppliers. This ensures they can monitor the amount owed by customers and take action to recover outstanding balances where necessary. They can also retain supplier goodwill by settling amounts due within the agreed time period.

The control account balances will appear in the trial balance at the period end and therefore, are ultimately included in the financial statements. Therefore, accuracy is very important.

For this reason, control account reconciliations are key as it enables businesses to identify discrepancies and then take action to remedy them.

1 Reasons for differences between the control account and the subsidiary ledgers

As was discussed in the previous chapter, if we add up the balances in the subsidiary sales and purchase ledgers, they should agree with the balances per the sales and purchase ledger control accounts.

If not, an error must have occurred at some point in the system.

In the assessment, having identified differences between the control account and respective ledger, you may be asked to identify the most likely reason(s) for the difference.

As you will have seen in the tasks above, there are many causes for the balance on the control accounts being different to the total of the ledger balances.

In general, differences are caused by:

- Only recording an item in the control account or ledger
- Over- or understating an item in the control account or ledger
- Duplicating an item in the control account or ledger
- Posting an item to the wrong side of the control account or ledger

To give some more specific examples:

The total balance of the sales ledger will be higher than the sales ledger control account if:

- A sales invoice has been duplicated in the sales ledger

- A cash receipt from a credit customer has been omitted from the sales ledger but recorded in the sales ledger control account

- A sales returns credit note has been omitted from the sales ledger but recorded in the sales ledger control account

The total balance of the sales ledger control account will be higher than the sales ledger if:

- Sales are recorded on the credit side of the sales ledger but posted correctly to the control account
- The total column in the sales day book has been overstated
- The total column showing bank receipts from credit customers has been understated
- Discounts allowed have been posted twice in the sales ledger but only once in the sales ledger control account

The total balance of the purchase ledger will be higher than the purchases ledger control account if:

- A purchases invoice has been duplicated in the purchases ledger
- A cash payment to a credit supplier has been omitted from the purchases ledger but is still included in the purchase ledger control account
- A purchases returns credit note has been omitted from the purchases ledger but recorded in the purchase ledger control account
- Discounts received have been omitted from the purchases ledger but recorded in the purchase ledger control account

The total balance of the purchase ledger control account will be higher than the purchase ledger if:

- Purchases are recorded on the debit side of the purchases ledger
- The total column in the purchases day book has been overstated
- The total column showing bank payments to credit suppliers has been understated
- Goods returned have been entered twice in the purchases ledger but only once in the purchase ledger control account

2 Assessment practice – control account reconciliations

Assessment focus point

In the assessment you could be asked to prepare a T account or tabular format and calculate the balance to be carried down/brought down. You may also be asked to calculate specific balances (such as the balance c/d or balance b/d).

In the next activities we will practise assessment standard tasks.

Activity 1: Sales ledger reconciliation – T account format

This is a summary of transactions with credit customers during March 20XX.

Transactions	Amount £
Balance of receivables at 1 March 20XX	28,566
Goods sold on credit	15,477
Money received from credit customers	20,451
Discount allowed	233
Goods returned by credit customers	1,543

(a) **Prepare a sales ledger control account from the details shown above. Show clearly the balance carried down at 31 March (closing balance) and brought down at 1 April (opening balance).**

Sales ledger control

Date 20XX	Details	Amount £	Date 20XX	Details	Amount £
1 MARCH	BALANCE b/d	28,566	31 MARCH	BANK	20,451
31 MAR	SALES	15,477		DISCOUNT ALLOWED	233.
				SALES RETURNS	1,543.
				Balance c/d	21,816.
		44013			44,043.
1 APRIL	BALANCE B/D	21,786			

Picklist:

Balance b/d ✓
Balance c/d ✓
Bank ✓
Discount allowed ✓
Sales ✓
Sales returns

The following balances were in the sales ledger on 1 April 20XX.

	£
ABC Ltd	5,409
Beavers UK	2,385
Caratons & Sons	10,877
Elisons Ltd	1,234
George M & Co	789
Halisom Ltd	549
Walter Bambride	806

(b) Reconcile the balances shown above with the sales ledger control account balance you have calculated in part (a).

	£
Sales ledger control account balance as at 1 April 20XX	21,816
Total of sales ledger accounts as at 1 April 20XX	22,049
Difference	233

(c) What could explain the difference you calculated in (b)? Tick ONE option.

Reasons	√
A sales invoice was duplicated in the sales ledger control account.	
The bank payment was not entered in the sales ledger control account.	
The total column of the sales day book was overstated.	
Discounts allowed were omitted from the sales ledger accounts.	√

Activity 2: Reconciling the sales ledger with the sales ledger control account

These are the accounts in the sales ledger at 1 September.

Harry and Co

Details	Amount £	Details	Amount £
Balance b/f	10,100		

Smith and sons

Details	Amount £	Details	Amount £
Balance b/f			530

William Ltd

Details	Amount £	Details	Amount £
Balance b/f	16,650		

Bernards plc

Details	Amount £	Details	Amount £
Balance b/f	25,980		

(a) **What is the total of the balances in the sales ledger on 1 September?**

£ | 52,200 ✓

The balance of the sales ledger control account on 1 September is £51,560.

(b) **What is the difference between the balance of the sales ledger control account and the total of the balances in the sales ledger you calculated in (a)?**

£ | 640 ✓

(c) **Which TWO of the reasons below could explain the difference you calculated in (b)?**

Reasons	√
Goods returned may have been entered in the sales ledger twice.	
Discounts allowed were entered on the debit side of the sales ledger control account.	
Goods sold were entered twice in a customer's account in the sales ledger.	✓
Goods returned were entered on the debit side of the sales ledger control account.	
A cheque received was omitted from the customer's account in the sales ledger.	✓
A cheque received was entered twice in a customer's account in the sales ledger.	

Activity 3: Purchases ledger reconciliation – T account format

This is a summary of transactions with credit suppliers during March 20XX.

Transactions	Amount £
Balance of payables at 1 March 20XX	15,732
Goods bought on credit	15,567
Payments made to credit suppliers (Bank)	13,731
Discount received	1,155
Goods returned to credit suppliers	2,251

(a) **Prepare a purchases ledger control account from the details shown above. Show clearly the balance carried down at 31 March (closing balance) and brought down at 1 April (opening balance).**

Purchases ledger control

Date 20XX	Details	Amount £	Date 20XX	Details	Amount £
31ST MARCH	BANK	13,731	1ST MAR 18	BALANCE BD	15,732
31ST MAR	DISCOUNT REC'D	1,155	31ST MAR	PURCHASES	15,567
31ST MAR	PURCHASES RETURNS	2,251			
31ST MAR	Balance c/d	14162			
		31,299			31,299
				Balance B/d	14,162

Picklist:

Balance b/d ✓
Balance c/d
Bank ✓
Discount received ✓
Purchases ✓
Purchases returns ✓

The following balances were in the purchases ledger on 1 April 20XX.

Transactions	Amount £
Albats Ltd	2,345
Boleys UK	1,150
Carosel Ltd	1,157
Kasey & Sons	557
Latherwaite	789
Samsons Ltd	7,998
Tramptons UK	2,417

(b) Reconcile the balances shown above with the purchases ledger control account balance you have calculated in part (a).

	£
Purchases ledger control account balance as at 1 April 20XX	14,162
Total of purchases ledger accounts as at 1 April 20XX	16,413
Difference	2,251

(c) **What may have caused the difference between the control account and ledger balances? Tick ONE option.**

Reasons	√
Goods returned may have been entered in the purchases ledger twice	
Goods returned may have been entered in the control account twice	✓
Discounts received may have been entered in the purchases ledger twice	
Discounts received may have been entered in the control account twice	

Activity 4: Purchases ledger reconciliation

At the beginning of April the following balances were in the purchases ledger:

| Details | Balances | |
	Amount £	Debit /Credit
LBW Ltd	20,143	Credit
G Roe	18,402	Credit
L Mann	8,677	Credit
M Williams	1,850	Debit
H Hope	12,942	Credit
G Gold	847	Credit

(a) **What should be the balance of the purchases ledger control account in order for it to reconcile with the total of the balances in the purchases ledger?**

	√
Debit balance b/d on 1 April of £59,161	
Credit balance b/d on 1 April of £59,161	✓
Debit balance b/d on 1 April of £62,861	
Credit balance b/d on 1 April of £62,861	

(b) Show whether the following are true or false.

Statements	True √	False √
The purchases ledger control account enables a business to identify how much is owed by credit customers in total.		√
The total balances in the purchases ledger should reconcile with the balances in the purchases ledger control account.	√	
A debit balance in the purchases ledger indicates a reduction in the total amount owed to credit suppliers.	√	

3 Credit control

One of the tasks of a credit controller (or credit control department) is to ensure that receivables pay on a timely basis and that any late payers are followed up promptly.

In order to follow up overdue invoices, the business must be able to identify overdue debts and determine how long customers take to pay.

A list of balances extracted from the sales ledger will tell us how much each customer owes but not how long the invoices have been outstanding for.

Sales ledger extract

Customer name	£
Bertrams	786
Florence	1,280
Quince	536
Titania	2,408
	5,010

The appropriate method of credit control, for example, a polite letter or one threatening legal action will depend on how overdue a debt has become.

From the example above we do not know if Florence always pays up and has only owed £1,280 for the past few days or if Titania Ltd has owed £2,408 for the past year.

In order to obtain sufficient information for credit control an aged receivables analysis must be prepared.

Example

Customer name	Credit limit £	Total balance £	Up to 30 days £	Up to 60 days £	Up to 90 days £	Over 90 days £
Bertrams	1,000	786	401	297	88	0
Florence	1,500	1,280	690	0	0	590
Quince	1,000	536	69	240	179	48
Titania	2,500	2,408	1,907	501	0	0
		5,010	3,067	1,038	267	638

This report analyses the balance owed by each customer according to the age of the invoice – ie how long it has been outstanding. This enables the appropriate action to be taken to collect the debt.

4 Irrecoverable debts

As we know, the balance brought down in the sales ledger control account is money due from customers. As it is something the business owns it represents an **asset**.

You are familiar with the concept that when a business sells on credit we record the invoice in the sales day book and that this is then posted to the main ledger using the following double entry:

Account name	Effect on elements	Debit √	Credit √
Sales ledger control	Increase in asset	√	
VAT	Increase in liability		√
Sales	Increase in income		√

The balance in the sales ledger control account can remain as an asset in the accounting records as long as the business believes it is recoverable, ie that the credit customer will pay. However, whenever a business sells on credit, there is always a risk that the customer may not pay for the goods/services provided.

Consequently, the business must review the balances owed from credit customers and identify items that are at significant risk of non-payment. This review is performed regularly, and in particular, when the financial statements are prepared.

Accounting treatment

If a business believes a debt is definitely irrecoverable, then it is no longer an asset of the business and should be written off. The journal entry is:

Account name	Effect on elements	Debit √	Credit √
Irrecoverable debt expenses	Increase in expenses	√	
VAT	Decrease in liability	√	
Sales ledger control	Decrease in asset		√

The next activity enables you to practise this journal.

Activity 5: Irrecoverable debts

A credit customer, Geraldine has ceased trading, owing Jessica Ltd £600 plus VAT at 20%.

Required

(a) **Record the journal entries needed in the general ledger to write off the net amount and the VAT.**

Account name	Amount £	Debit √	Credit √
IRRecoverable debt expenses	600	√	
VAT	120	√	
SLCA	720		√

Another credit customer, DD Dayton has ceased trading, owing Jessica Ltd £5,400 including VAT at 20%.

(b) **Record the journal entries needed in the general ledger to write off the net amount and the VAT.**

Account name	Amount £	Debit √	Credit √
Irrecoverable debt expenses	4500	√	
VAT	900	√	
SLCA	5400		√

Picklist:

Irrecoverable debt expenses
Sales
Sales ledger control
VAT

BPP
LEARNING MEDIA

Assessment focus point

In the assessment you are likely to be required to write off an irrecoverable debt. Therefore, make sure you are able to record this journal in the general ledger.

Chapter summary

- If all of the entries in the general ledger are correctly made, then the totals of the closing balances on the subsidiary sales and purchases ledgers should agree with the balances on the relevant control accounts.

- If the entries in the general ledger and sales and purchases ledgers have not been properly made, then the total of these ledger balances will not agree with the balances on the control accounts – in which case, the causes of the difference must be investigated.

- A sales ledger control account reconciliation compares the balance on the sales ledger control account with the total of the balances in the sales ledger. Both are amended for any errors that have been made, so the balance and the total should be the same after putting through the amendments.

- A purchases ledger control account reconciliation works in exactly the same way as the sales ledger control account reconciliation, although all of the entries and balances are on the opposite sides.

- An aged trade receivables analysis is used to monitor how slowly customers are paying their debts, and to make decisions about how/when to chase for payment.

- The double entry for writing off an irrecoverable debt is to debit the irrecoverable debts expense account and the VAT control account, and credit the sales ledger control account.

Keywords

- **Aged trade receivables analysis:** A schedule showing, for each credit customer, how long the component parts of the balance have been unpaid

- **Irrecoverable debt:** A debt which it is believed will never be recovered

- **Purchases ledger control account reconciliation:** An exercise that agrees the balance on the purchases ledger control account with the total of the list of balances in the purchases ledger

- **Sales ledger control account reconciliation:** An exercise that agrees the balance on the sales ledger control account with the total of the list of balances in the sales ledger

- **Writing off:** Removing an irrecoverable debt from the ledger accounts

Activity 1: Sales ledger reconciliation – T account format

(a) **Prepare a sales ledger control account from the details shown above. Show clearly the balance carried down at 31 March (closing balance) and brought down at 1 April (opening balance).**

Sales ledger control

Date 20XX	Details	Amount £	Date 20XX	Details	Amount £
1 March	Balance b/d	28,566	31 March	Bank	20,451
31 March	Sales	15,477	31 March	Discount allowed	233
			31 March	Sales returns	1,543
			31 March	Balance c/d	21,816
		44,043			44,043
1 April	Balance b/d	21,816			

(b) **Reconcile the balances shown above with the sales ledger control account balance you have calculated in part (a).**

	Amount £
Sales ledger control account balance as at 1 April 20XX	21,816
Total of sales ledger accounts as at 1 April 20XX	22,049
Difference	233

(c)   What could explain the difference you calculated in (b)? Tick ONE option.

Reasons	√
A sales invoice was duplicated in the sales ledger control account.	
The bank payment was not entered in the sales ledger control account.	
The total column of the sales day book was overstated.	
Discounts allowed were omitted from the sales ledger accounts.	√

The total of the subsidiary sales ledger accounts is higher than the sales ledger control account. Discounts allowed decrease the sales ledger balance, and therefore omitting them from the sales ledger accounts would cause this balance to be higher than the balance b/d in the sales ledger control account. Therefore, statement 4 is correct.

The other statements are incorrect. Duplicating a sales invoice in the sales ledger control account would cause this balance to be higher than the sales ledger accounts. Omitting the bank payment from the sales ledger control account would also cause this balance to be higher than the total of the subsidiary sales ledger accounts. Also, overstating the total column of the sales day book would cause the sales ledger control account to be higher than the total of the subsidiary sales ledger accounts.

Activity 2: Reconciling the sales ledger with the sales ledger control account

(a)   What is the total of the balances in the sales ledger on 1 September?

£	52,200

The balance of the sales ledger control account on 1 September is £51,560.

(b)   What is the difference between the balance of the sales ledger control account and the total of the balances in the sales ledger you calculated in (a)?

£	640

(c) Which TWO of the reasons below could explain the difference you calculated in (b)?

Reasons	√
Goods returned may have been entered in the sales ledger twice.	
Discounts allowed were entered on the debit side of the sales ledger control account.	
Goods sold were entered twice in a customer's account in the sales ledger.	√
Goods returned were entered on the debit side of the sales ledger control account.	
A cheque received was omitted from the customer's account in the sales ledger.	√
A cheque received was entered twice in a customer's account in the sales ledger.	

The total of the subsidiary sales ledger balances is higher than the sales ledger control account balance.

Statements 3 and 5 – this could be caused by a sales invoice being entered twice in a customer's account in the sales ledger, as this would increase the total of the subsidiary sales ledger balances. Also, a cheque received from a credit customer reduces the asset as the customer is settling an amount owed. Therefore, omitting it from a customer's account would cause the total of the subsidiary sales ledger balance to be higher than the sales ledger control account balance.

Statements 1 and 6 – duplicating goods returned and a cheque received from a credit customer in the sales ledger would cause the total of the subsidiary sales ledger balances to be lower than the control account, hence they cannot be valid reasons here.

Statements 2 and 4 – including discounts allowed and goods returned on the debit side of the sales ledger control account would cause this balance to be higher than the total of the subsidiary sales ledger balance. This is not the case here, therefore, they do not explain the difference in this scenario.

Activity 3: Purchases ledger reconciliation – T account format

(a) **Prepare a purchases ledger control account from the details shown above. Show clearly the balance carried down at 31 March (closing balance) and brought down at 1 April (opening balance).**

Purchases ledger control

Date 20XX	Details	Amount £	Date 20XX	Details	Amount £
31 March	Bank	13,731	1 March	Balance b/d	15,732
31 March	Discount received	1,155	31 March	Purchases	15,567
31 March	Purchases returns	2,251			
31 March	Balance c/d	14,162			
		31,299			31,299
			1 April	Balance b/d	14,162

(b) **Reconcile the balances shown above with the purchases ledger control account balance you have calculated in part (a).**

	Amount £
Purchases ledger control account balance as at 1 April 20XX	14,162
Total of purchases ledger accounts as at 1 April 20XX	16,413
Difference	2,251

(c) **What may have caused the difference between the control account and ledger balances? Tick ONE option.**

Reasons	√
Goods returned may have been entered in the purchases ledger twice.	
Goods returned may have been entered in the control account twice.	√
Discounts received may have been entered in the purchases ledger twice.	
Discounts received may have been entered in the control account twice.	

The total of the purchases ledger control account is lower than the subsidiary purchases ledger total by £2,251. Discounts received and goods returned both reduce the liability to credit suppliers, therefore, the duplication of the entry must have occurred in the purchases ledger control account. The information in the scenario shows purchases returns as being £2,251, hence the difference is most likely to relate to the duplication of this item.

Activity 4: Purchases ledger reconciliation

(a) What should be the balance of the purchases ledger control account in order for it to reconcile with the total of the balances in the purchases ledger?

	√
Debit balance b/d on 1 April of £59,161	
Credit balance b/d on 1 April of £59,161	√
Debit balance b/d on 1 April of £62,861	
Credit balance b/d on 1 April of £62,861	

(b) Show whether the following are true or false.

Statements	True √	False √
The purchases ledger control account enables a business to identify how much is owed by credit customers in total.		√
The total balances in the purchases ledger should reconcile with the balances in the purchases ledger control account.	√	
A debit balance in the purchases ledger indicates a reduction in the total amount owed to credit suppliers.	√	

Statement 1 – the purchases ledger control account enables a business to identify how much is owed by credit suppliers in total, not credit customers. Statements 2 and 3 are correct.

Activity 5: Irrecoverable debts

(a) Record the journal entries needed in the general ledger to write off the net amount and the VAT.

Account name	Amount £	Debit √	Credit √
Irrecoverable debt expenses	600	√	
VAT	120	√	
Sales ledger control	720		√

(b) Record the journal entries needed in the general ledger to write off the net amount and the VAT.

Account name	Amount £	Debit √	Credit √
Irrecoverable debt expenses	4,500	√	
VAT	900	√	
Sales ledger control	5,400		√

Note that scenario (a) is exclusive of the VAT, therefore the VAT is calculated as £600 x 20% = £120. The gross total posted to the sales ledger control account is £600 + £120 = £720.

Whereas, the VAT inclusive amount is given in scenario (b). Therefore, the VAT is calculated as £5,400 x 20/120 = £900. The net total posted to the irrecoverable debt expense account is calculated as £5,400 – £900 = £4,500.

1   **Indicate whether the following statement is true or false.**

Statement	True ✓	False ✓
An aged receivables analysis is a schedule showing, for each credit customer, how long the component parts of the balance have been unpaid.	✓	

2   The balance on a business's sales ledger control account at the end of June was £40,500 and the total of the list of balances in the sales ledger came to £40,250.

Which of the following could explain the difference?

Statements	✓
The sales day book was undercast by £250 on one page.	
An invoice for £250 was omitted from the sales ledger account.	✓
A discount allowed to a customer of £250 was posted to the debit side of the sales ledger account.	
Cash received of £250 was only posted to the sales ledger control account.	

3   A credit customer, John & Co has ceased trading, owing Hopkins £1,200 plus VAT at 20%. **Record the journal entries needed in the general ledger to write off the net amount and the VAT.**

Account name	Amount £	Debit ✓	Credit ✓
Irrecover	1440		✓
SLC	1200	✓	
VAT	240	✓	

Picklist:

Irrecoverable debt expenses
Sales ledger control
VAT

4 One of Grangemouth Ltd's credit customers, Markham & Co, has ceased trading, owing Grangemouth Ltd £1,290 plus VAT.

Using the picklist, record the journal entries needed in the general ledger to write off the net amount and the VAT.

Account name	Amount £	Debit ✓	Credit ✓
Sales	1290	✓	
VAT	258	✓	
Irrec.	1548		✓

Picklist:

Irrecoverable debts
Sales
Sales ledger control
VAT

5 This is a summary of transactions with suppliers during the month of August.

(a) **Show whether each entry will be a debit or credit in the purchases ledger control account in the general ledger.**

Details	Amount £	Debit ✓	Credit ✓
Amount due to credit suppliers at 1 August	42,394		✓
Payments to credit suppliers	39,876	✓	
Purchases on credit	31,243		✓
Purchases returned to credit suppliers	1,266		✓
Discounts received	501	✓	

(b) **What will be the balance brought forward on 1 September on the above account?**

7490
40 377

	✓
Debit £31,994	
Credit £31,994	
Debit £34,526	
Credit £34,526	✓
Debit £32,996	
Credit £32,996	

(c) The following credit balances were in the purchases ledger on 1 September.

	Amount £
Robinson Kate	8,239
Livesley Ltd	6,300
Townsend and Douglas	1,204
Miles Better Co	10,993
Strongarm Partners	4,375
Ambley Brothers	1,079

Reconcile the balances shown above with the purchases ledger control account balance you have calculated in part (b).

	Amount £
Purchases ledger control account balance as at 31 August	34 526
Total of purchases ledger accounts as at 31 August	32 190
Difference	2336

(d) What may have caused the difference you calculated in part (c)?

Reasons	✓
A debit balance in the purchases ledger may have been included as a credit balance when calculating the total of the list of balances	
A credit balance in the purchases ledger may have been included as a debit balance when calculating the total of the list of balances	
A credit note may have been omitted from the purchases returns day book total	
Discounts received may only have been entered in the purchases ledger	

The journal

5

Learning outcomes

Having studied this chapter you will be able to:

2.3	Identify the purpose of the journal
	• The purpose of the journal as a book of prime entry
	• Transactions that are recorded in the journal:
	– Opening entries for a new business
	– Payroll transactions
4.1	**Produce journal entries to record accounting transactions**
	• Record opening entries for a new business
	• Identify and record entries for payroll transactions:
	– Wages control account
	– Gross pay
	– Income tax
	– Employer's and employees' national insurance contributions (NIC)
	– Employer's and employees' pension and voluntary deductions.

Assessment context

We have been preparing journal entries since we first looked at double entry in *Bookkeeping transactions*. We now take this further by studying other transactions that businesses record by way of journal entry. In particular, preparing opening entries for a new business and payroll transactions are important areas of the syllabus.

Qualification context

In the level 3 accounting units you will record journal entries for many accounting transactions including items introduced in the *Advanced bookkeeping unit* such as accruals, prepayments and depreciation. In *Financial statements for limited companies* you will process journals as you prepare the accounts.

Business context

Journal entries are necessary to prepare accurate, complete and reliable accounts which are used by company owners to assist with business decisions.

Chapter overview

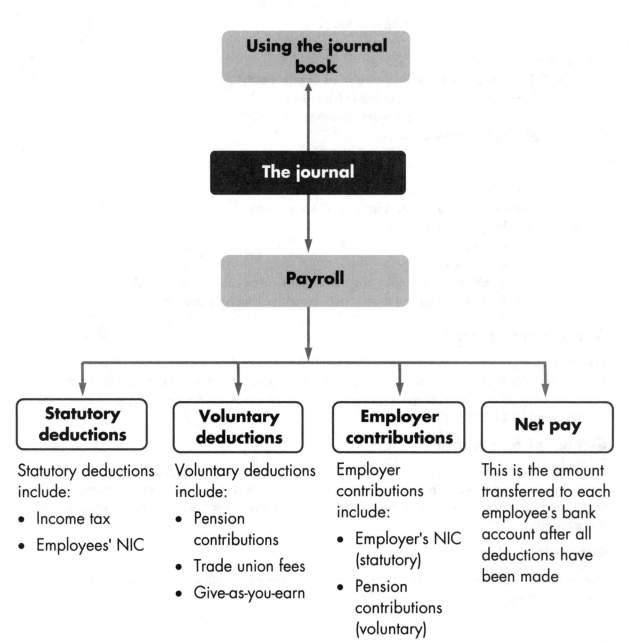

Use of the journal book includes:

- Entering opening balances in a new set of ledger accounts
- Recording payroll transactions

Using the journal book

The journal

Payroll

Statutory deductions

Statutory deductions include:

- Income tax
- Employees' NIC

Voluntary deductions

Voluntary deductions include:

- Pension contributions
- Trade union fees
- Give-as-you-earn

Employer contributions

Employer contributions include:

- Employer's NIC (statutory)
- Pension contributions (voluntary)

Net pay

This is the amount transferred to each employee's bank account after all deductions have been made

Introduction

Once the initial trial balance has been drawn up it will be reviewed to identify further adjustments that are needed before the accounts can be prepared.

These adjustments are recorded in a book of prime entry known as the journal book.

The journal book is used to record transactions that do not appear in any of the other books of prime entry, so they can then be posted to the ledgers.

For your assessment you need to be able to post journal entries to:

- Write off irrecoverable debts (seen in the previous chapter)
- Enter opening balances in a new set of ledger accounts
- Record payroll transactions
- Correct errors (studied in the next chapter)

1 Journal entries

The journal consists of a series of journal entries. A journal entry is a written instruction to the bookkeeper to enter the transactions in the ledger.

Illustration 1: Journal entry

Journal number	0225	
Date	5 April 20XX	
Authorised by	D Fisher	
Account	R Sanderson	
Account name	**Debit £**	**Credit £**
Irrecoverable debts expense	700.00	
VAT control	140.00	
Sales ledger control		840.00
Total	840.00	840.00

Narrative: being to record an irrecoverable debt write off in the nominal ledger.

Points to note:

- The amounts to be entered in each ledger account are set out, and whether they are to be debited or credited.

- A total is calculated for debits and for credits, to check that the amounts are the same and in turn, that the double entry is correct.

In your assessment, you would show this journal, as far as it affects the general ledger, as follows:

Account name	Amount £	Debit ✓	Credit ✓
Irrecoverable debts expense	700.00	✓	
VAT control	140.00	✓	
Sales ledger control	840.00		✓

In the assessment, you may also need to prepare a journal for the sales ledger:

Account name	Amount £	Debit ✓	Credit ✓
R Sanderson	840.00		✓

Assessment focus point

In the assessment you choose the account name from a given picklist of names, you enter the figure in the 'amount' column, and then you place a tick in the debit or credit column as appropriate. Note that you will **not** have to provide a narrative explanation of the journal in the assessment.

2 Journal to record opening entries for a new business

Journals are used to open the accounting records for new businesses.

Entering opening asset, liability and capital balances

To enter the business's assets, liabilities and capital in the new set of accounts:

- Asset accounts are entered as debit balances
- Liability and capital accounts are entered as credit balances

Illustration 2: Opening journal

Sarah Clifford is starting a business on 1 November 20XX with the following balances:

	£
Bank loan	22,000
Capital	10,000
Cash at bank	6,550
Non-current assets	25,000
Petty cash	450

We need to create a journal to enter the appropriate opening balances in Sarah's accounts, as at 1 November 20XX.

To do this, first work through the list identifying balances as debits or credits.

Journal

Account name	Debit £	Credit £
Bank loan		22,000
Capital		10,000
Cash at bank	6,550	
Non-current assets	25,000	
Petty cash	450	
Totals	32,000	32,000

Next, the journal entry is posted to a new nominal ledger.

Bank loan

Details	Amount £	Details	Amount £
		Journal	22,000

Capital

Details	Amount £	Details	Amount £
		Journal	10,000

Cash at bank

Details	Amount £	Details	Amount £
Journal	6,550		

Non-current assets

Details	Amount £	Details	Amount £
Journal	25,000		

Petty cash

Details	Amount £	Details	Amount £
Journal	450		

Assessment focus point

As you will see in the next activity, in your assessment you will be asked to record the opening journal entries for a new business. It is important to know whether the amounts in each account need to be included in the debit or credit columns.

Activity 1: Opening journal for a new business

Castle Timbers has started a new business, Castle Irons, and a new set of accounts are to be opened. A partially completed journal to record the opening entries is shown below.

Required

Record the journal entries needed in the accounts in the general ledger of Castle Irons to deal with the opening entries.

Account name	Amount £	Debit √	Credit √
Cash at bank	132,000	√	
Capital	100,000		√
Motor vehicle	18,000	√	
Loan from bank	50,000		√

3 Payroll

3.1 Introduction to payroll

Salaries and wages usually form a substantial part of a business's expenditure, especially in service organisations. However, salaries and wages expenditure does not arise in the same way as other cash and credit purchases.

The entries in the accounting system that are made in respect of salaries and wages are known as **payroll transactions**. To understand these, you need to have a basic understanding of the main statutory and voluntary transactions which are processed through payroll.

Assessment focus point

Note that for this assessment, you do not need to know how to calculate tax; instead, the focus is on posting the journal entries to record payroll transactions.

Gross pay

Gross pay is the total amount that the employer owes the employee before any deductions have been made.

Statutory deductions

Income tax (pay-as-you-earn or PAYE) and employees' NIC are known as statutory deductions from gross pay, because the law (statute) requires employers to make these deductions from individuals' salaries.

Employees pay their income tax under the PAYE system. This means that each time an employee is paid by their employer, the income tax for that period (eg monthly) is deducted from their wages by the employer. At regular intervals the employer then pays the income tax over to the tax collecting authority on the employees' behalf. In the UK the tax collecting authority is Her Majesty's Revenue & Customs (HMRC).

Employees must also pay employees' national insurance contributions (NIC) to HMRC. NIC is just another form of tax, calculated differently from income tax. An individual employee's NIC are deducted from the employee's wages and paid over to HMRC, together with the employee's income tax.

Voluntary deductions

An employee may choose to have other (voluntary) deductions made from gross pay. These items can only be deducted from an employee's gross salary **if** the employer has the employee's written permission to do so.

For example, if an employee chooses to make pension contributions, this money is deducted from gross pay and transferred to a pension administrator to provide a pension for the employee on retirement. Other voluntary deductions include trade union fees and give-as-you-earn (GAYE).

Net pay

Once all deductions have been made, the amount paid to the employee is called net pay.

It is sometimes referred to as 'take home pay'.

Employer's national insurance contribution (statutory)

The employer is also required to pay an additional amount of NIC for each employee, known as the employer's NIC. This is yet another form of tax, but the difference is that it is only suffered by the employer. There is no deduction from the employee's gross pay for the employer's NIC. Employer's NIC is paid by the employer to HMRC.

Employer's pension contribution (voluntary)

The employer may make a voluntary contribution to the employee's pension. Again, this is in addition to the gross pay. Therefore, it increases the 'total cost' of employing individuals. However, it is not deducted from the gross pay.

Illustration 3: Payroll transactions

Let us suppose that Ian is employed by Southfield. He earns £48,000 a year which is paid monthly. This means that each month his gross pay is (£48,000/12) = £4,000.

Remember, gross pay is the amount an employee earns before any deductions are made.

And, the gross amount also excludes any employer contributions made in addition to gross pay (such as employer's national insurance and pension contributions).

Statutory deductions

The payroll department of Southfield has calculated that the income tax due by Ian for this month is £770, and that his employees' NIC payment for the month should be £320.

Therefore, after statutory deductions have been made, so far Ian's monthly net pay is calculated as follows:

Item	Amount £	Paid by Southfield to:
Gross wages	4,000	
Income tax	(770)	HM Revenue and Customs
NIC	(320)	HM Revenue and Customs
Net pay	2,910	Ian

Voluntary deduction (pension contribution)

When Ian joined Southfield, it was agreed that each month he would pay £200 per month into the company pension scheme and Southfield would make a further contribution of £300 to the pension scheme.

Therefore, after statutory deductions and the employee's pension contribution have been made, so far Ian's monthly net pay is calculated as follows:

Item	Amount £	Paid by Southfield to:
Gross pay	4,000	
Income tax	(770)	HM Revenue and Customs
Employees' NIC	(320)	HM Revenue and Customs
Pension contribution	(200)	Pension scheme
Net pay	2,710	Ian

So of the original gross wages of £4,000 per month, Ian only receives £2,710. However, the amount of income tax that he owed has been paid, as has the amount of NIC due from him, and he has also paid into his pension fund.

Employer's national insurance and employer's pension contributions

There are two further payments for Southfield to make. As we have seen, they have a statutory obligation to pay employer's national insurance contributions. This is £415 for Ian.

And they are making a voluntary contribution to Ian's pension of £300. In summary:

Type of payment	Amount £	Paid by Southfield to:
Employer's NIC	415	HMRC
Employer's pension	300	Pension scheme

Therefore, the total cost to Southfield of employing Ian each month is:

Item	Amount £
Gross pay	4,000
Employer's NIC	415
Employer's pension	300
	4,715

3.2 Full cost of employing an employee

Where employer's pension contributions are made, the full cost of employing an employee is:

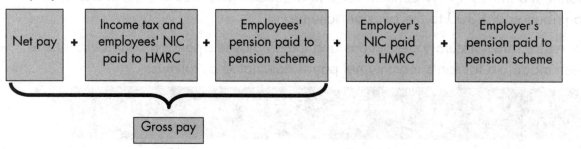

Therefore, gross pay plus employer's NIC plus employer's pension contribution is the cost of employing employees and what appears as the wages expense for the business.

3.3 Accounting for payroll

Payroll is accounted for using the double entry bookkeeping rules that we are familiar with. There are, however, some new ledger (or T) accounts which are used for this purpose.

In this assessment, payroll transactions are recorded using a wages control account. Therefore, when payroll expenses occur, the liability is initially credited to this account.

Account name	Purpose
Wages control	This is like any other control account and helps ensure that the double entry is made correctly. All payroll liabilities are initially credited to this control account. They are subsequently transferred to the relevant nominal ledger account (such as HMRC, pension and bank).
Wages expense	This expense account shows the total cost to the business of employing someone (ie the gross salary **plus** the employer's NIC and if applicable, the employer's pension contribution).
HM Revenue and Customs	This liability account shows the amount of income tax and NIC owed to the tax authorities.
Pension	This liability account shows the amount of pension that must be paid over to the pension scheme. It will include both the employees' and employer's contributions.

Note that there may be other payable accounts if further voluntary deductions are made, say in respect of trade union fees and give-as-you-earn (GAYE).

There are a number of double entries to be made:

(i) Gross pay is recorded:

Account name	Debit √	Credit √
Wages expense	√	
Wages control		√

(ii) Net pay is paid to employees:

Account name	Debit √	Credit √
Wages control	√	
Bank		√

(iii) Income tax and employees' NIC is allocated to the HM Revenue and Customs account:

Account name	Debit √	Credit √
Wages control	√	
HM Revenue and Customs		√

(iv) Employees' pension contributions are allocated to the pension account:

Account name	Debit √	Credit √
Wages control	√	
Pension		√

(v) Employer's NIC is recorded:

Account name	Debit √	Credit √
Wages expense	√	
Wages control		√

(vi) Employer's NIC is transferred to the HMRC account:

Account name	Debit √	Credit √
Wages control	√	
HM Revenue and Customs		√

(vii) Employer's pension contributions are recorded:

Account name	Debit √	Credit √
Wages expense	√	
Wages control		√

(viii) Employer's pension contribution is transferred to the pension account:

Account name	Debit √	Credit √
Wages control	√	
Pension		√

Illustration 4: Accounting for payroll

We return to Ian's wages payment which is summarised below:

	£
Gross wages	4,000
Income tax	(770)
Employee's NIC	(320)
Employee's pension contribution	(200)
Net pay	2,710
Employer's NIC	415
Employer's pension contribution	300

The entries in the ledger accounts are as follows:

(i)   Gross pay of £4,000 is recorded:

Wages expense

Details	Amount £	Details	Amount £
Wages control (i)	4,000		

Wages control

Details	Amount £	Details	Amount £
		Wages expense (i)	4,000

(ii)   Net pay of £2,710 is paid to the employee:

Wages control

Details	Amount £	Details	Amount £
Bank (ii)	2,710	Wages expense (i)	4,000

Bank

Details	Amount £	Details	Amount £
		Wages control (ii)	2,710

(iii) Income tax of £770 and employee's NIC of £320 is allocated to the HM Revenue and Customs account:

Wages control

Details	Amount £	Details	Amount £
Bank (ii)	2,710	Wages expense (i)	4,000
HM Revenue and Customs (770 + 320) (iii)	1,090		

HM Revenue and Customs

Details	Amount £	Details	Amount £
		Wages control (iii)	1,090

(iv) Employee's pension contribution of £200 is allocated to the pension account:

Wages control

Details	Amount £	Details	Amount £
Bank (ii)	2,710	Wages expense (i)	4,000
HM Revenue and Customs (770 + 320) (iii)	1,090		
Pension (iv)	200		

Pension

Details	Amount £	Details	Amount £
		Wages control (iv)	200

(v) Employer's NIC of £415 is recorded and then (vi) the liability is transferred to the HM Revenue and Customs account:

Wages control

Details	Amount £	Details	Amount £
Bank (ii)	2,710	Wages expense (i)	4,000
HM Revenue and Customs (iii)	1,090	Wages expense (v)	415
Pension (iv)	200		
HM Revenue and Customs (vi)	415		

Wages expense

Details	Amount £	Details	Amount £
Wages control (i)	4,000		
Wages control (v)	415		

HM Revenue and Customs

Details	Amount £	Details	Amount £
		Wages control (iii)	1,090
		Wages control (vi)	415

(vii) Employer's pension contribution of £300 recorded and then (viii) the liability is transferred to the HM Revenue and Customs account

This is the final time we see the wages control account in this illustration. As a check that the double entry is correct, note that if we total the account there is no balance c/d. This suggests the payroll entries are correct.

Wages control

Details	Amount £	Details	Amount £
Bank (ii)	2,710	Wages expense (i)	4,000
HM Revenue and Customs (iii)	1,090	Wages expense (v)	415
Pension (iv)	200	Wages expense (vii)	300
HM Revenue and Customs (vi)	415		
Pension (viii)	300		
	4,715		4,715

Wages expense

Details	Amount £	Details	Amount £
Wages control (i)	4,000		
Wages control (v)	415		
Wages control (vii)	300		

Pension

Details	Amount £	Details	Amount £
		Wages control (iv)	200
		Wages control (viii)	300

The illustration suggests that accounting for payroll involves many journals. However, the essential principle is to:

*   Debit the wages expense with the total cost (this is an expense, hence the debit entry)

*   Credit the wages control account with the liability (an increase in liabilities is entered on the credit side of the T account)

- Then, 'reallocate' amounts owed from the wages control account to the relevant liability account (HMRC, pension etc) and transfer the net pay to the individual (bank).

Assessment focus point

In the exam you will record payroll journals in the ledger, using a wages control account. Therefore, it is very important to learn the double entries required to enter each payroll transaction.

Activity 2: Accounting for payroll – HH Co

HH Co pays its employees by cheque every month and maintains a wages control account. A summary of last month's payroll transactions is shown below.

Item	Amount £
Gross pay	60,000
Employees' NI	2,000
Income tax	8,000
Employer's NI	4,000

Required

(a) **Record the above information in the main ledger accounts.**

GENERAL LEDGER

Wages expense

Details	Amount £	Details	Amount £

Wages control

Details	Amount £	Details	Amount £

Bank

Details	Amount £	Details	Amount £
Balance b/f	100,000		

HM Revenue and Customs

Details	Amount £	Details	Amount £

Picklist:

Bank
HM Revenue and Customs
Pension
Wages control
Wages expense

Complete the following sentences.

(b)	The total cost to the business of employing staff is	£	

(c)	The business owes	£		to HM Revenue and Customs.

The above activity considers accounting for payroll transactions when only legal deductions occur. The next activity requires you to record payroll transactions with the additional consideration of payroll contributions.

Activity 3: Accounting for payroll – SMB Co

SMB Co pays its employees by cheque every month and maintains a wages control account. A summary of last month's payroll transactions is shown below.

Item	Amount £
Gross pay	9,452
Employees' NI	842
Income tax	1,305
Employees' pension contributions	140
Employer's NI	1,042

(a) Record the wages expense

Account name	Amount £	Debit √	Credit √

(b) Record the HM Revenue and Customs liability

Account name	Amount £	Debit √	Credit √

(c) Record the net wages paid to the employees

Account name	Amount £	Debit √	Credit √

(d) Record the pension payable

Account name	Amount £	Debit √	Credit √

Picklist:

Bank
Employees NI
Employers NI
HM Revenue and Customs
Income tax
Net wages
Pension
Wages control
Wages expense

Activity 4: Accounting for payroll – Stanley

Stanley pays its employees by cheque every month and maintains a wages control account. A summary of last month's payroll transactions is shown below.

Item	Amount £
Gross pay	11,352
Employees' NI	901
Income tax	1,652
Employer's pension contributions	245
Employer's NI	1,241

(a) Record the wages expense

Account name	Amount £	Debit √	Credit √

(b) Record the HM Revenue and Customs liability

Account name	Amount £	Debit √	Credit √

(c)   Record the net wages paid to the employees

Account name	Amount £	Debit √	Credit √

(d)   Record the pension payable

Account name	Amount £	Debit √	Credit √

Picklist:

Bank
Employees NI
Employers NI
HM Revenue and Customs
Income tax
Net wages
Pension
Wages control
Wages expense

Chapter summary

- The journal book is used to record transactions that do not appear in any of the other books of prime entry, so they can then be posted to the ledgers. This includes:

  - opening entries for a new business
  - payroll transactions

- When recording the opening entries for a new business, asset balances must be posted to the debit side of the ledger. Liability and capital balances are posted to the credit side of the ledger.

- The total payroll cost is the employees' gross pay plus employer's NIC plus where applicable, employer's pension contributions.

- Income tax and employees' national insurance contributions (NIC) must be deducted from an employee's gross pay.

- Voluntary deductions may also made, for example, employee pension contributions, trade union fees and give-as-you-earn (GAYE).

- Accounting for payroll involves the use of several nominal ledger accounts:

  - Wages control account
  - Wages expense account
  - HM Revenue and Customs account
  - Pension account
  - Other payable accounts if further voluntary deductions are made

Keywords

- **Gross pay:** The salary/wages payable to an employee before any statutory or voluntary deductions

- **Her Majesty's Revenue & Customs (HMRC):** The UK government department responsible for collecting tax

- **Income tax:** A tax that is paid by individuals on all sources of income, including salary/wages

- **Journal book:** The journal book is used to record transactions that do not appear in any of the other books of prime entry, so they can then be posted to the ledgers

- **Journal entry:** A written instruction to the bookkeeper to make a double entry into the ledgers

- **National insurance contributions (employees' NIC) :** A tax on employees' income deducted from gross pay

- **National insurance contributions (employer's NIC):** An additional tax, suffered by the employer, based on an employee's gross pay

- **Net pay:** The amount of the employee's wages actually paid to the employee, net of statutory and voluntary deductions

- **Payroll transactions:** Payments to employees in respect of salaries and wages

- **Pension contribution:** A form of voluntary deduction from employees, and a contribution from employers which is paid to the pension administrator to provide a pension for the employee on retirement

- **Statutory deductions:** Deductions that must be made by the employer from an employee's pay in respect of income tax and employees' NIC

- **Voluntary deductions:** Non-statutory amounts deducted from employees' pay with their consent eg Give-As-You-Earn (GAYE) and trade union subscriptions

- **Wages control account:** This is like any other control account and helps ensure that the double entry is made correctly

Activity answers

Activity 1: Opening journal for a new business

Record the journal entries needed in the accounts in the general ledger of Castle Irons to deal with the opening entries.

Account name	Amount £	Debit √	Credit √
Cash at bank	132,000	√	
Capital	100,000		√
Motor vehicle	18,000	√	
Loan from bank	50,000		√

Activity 2: Accounting for payroll – HH Co

(a) Record the above information in the general ledger accounts.

Wages expense

Details	Amount £	Details	Amount £
Wages control	60,000		
Wages control	4,000		

Wages control

Details	Amount £	Details	Amount £
Bank	50,000	Wages expense	60,000
HM Revenue and Customs	8,000	Wages expense	4,000
HM Revenue and Customs	2,000		
HM Revenue and Customs	4,000		

Bank

Details	Amount £	Details	Amount £
Balance b/f	100,000	Wages control	50,000

HM Revenue and Customs

Details	Amount £	Details	Amount £
		Wages control	8,000
		Wages control	2,000
		Wages control	4,000

Complete the following sentences.

(b)	The total cost to the business of employing staff is	£	64,000

Tutorial note

The total cost is the gross salaries **plus** the employers NIC. Therefore, £60,000 + £4,000 = £64,000

(c)	The business owes	£	14,000	to HM Revenue and Customs.

Tutorial note

The business needs to pay the PAYE, employees NIC and employers NIC over to HMRC.

£8,000 + £2,000 + £4,000 = £14,000

Activity 3: Accounting for payroll – SMB Co

(a) Record the wages expense

Account name	Amount £	Debit √	Credit √
Wages expense	10,494	√	
Wages control	10,494		√

Working: £9,452 + £1,042 = £10,494

(b) Record the HRMC liability

Account name	Amount £	Debit √	Credit √
Wages control	3,189	√	
HM Revenue and Customs	3,189		√

Working: £842 + £1,305 + £1,042 = £3,189

(c) Record the net wages paid to the employees

Account name	Amount £	Debit √	Credit √
Wages control	7,165	√	
Bank	7,165		√

Working: £9,452 – £842 – £1,305 – £140 = £7,165

(d) Record the pension payable

Account name	Amount £	Debit √	Credit √
Wages control	140	√	
Pension	140		√

Activity 4: Accounting for payroll – Stanley

(a) Record the wages expense

Account name	Amount £	Debit √	Credit √
Wages expense	12,838	√	
Wages control	12,838		√

Working: £11,352 + £245 + £1,241 = £12,838

(b) Record the HM Revenue and Customs liability

Account name	Amount £	Debit √	Credit √
Wages control	3,794	√	
HM Revenue and Customs	3,794		√

Working: £901 + £1,652 + £1,241 = £3,794

(c) Record the net wages paid to the employees

Account name	Amount £	Debit √	Credit √
Wages control	8,799	√	
Bank	8,799		√

Working: £11,352 – £901 – £1,652 = £8,799

(d) Record the pension payable

Account name	Amount £	Debit √	Credit √
Wages control	245	√	
Pension	245		√

Test your learning

1   A new business, Carswell & Sons, is opening a new set of accounts. A partially completed journal to record the opening entries is shown below.

Record the journal entries needed in the accounts in the general ledger of Carswell & Sons to deal with the opening entries.

Account name	Amount £	Debit ✓	Credit ✓
Capital	28,000		
Cash at bank	21,000		
Loan from bank	5,000		
Machinery	12,000		

2   An employee earns a gross salary of £27,000 per year and is paid on a monthly basis. For the month of October, the payroll department has calculated an income tax deduction of £418.16 and NI contributions due of £189.00 from the employee and £274.50 from the employer.

What is the employee's net pay?

£

3   **State whether the following deductions from gross pay are statutory or voluntary deductions:**

	Statutory deduction ✓	Voluntary deduction ✓
Pension contributions		
Income tax		
Employee's NIC		
Trade union fees		

4   **Indicate whether the following statements are true or false.**

	True ✓	False ✓
Employer's NIC are deducted from gross pay.		
Employer's pension contributions are in addition to gross pay.		

5 A business pays its employees by BACS every month and maintains a wages control account. A summary of last month's payroll transactions is shown below:

Item	Amount £
Gross wages	12,756
Employer's NIC	1,020
Employees' NIC	765
Income tax	1,913
Trade union liability	100

Using the picklist, record the journal entries needed in the general ledger to:

(a) Record the wages expense

Account name	Amount £	Debit ✓	Credit ✓

(b) Record the amount payable to HM Revenue and Customs

Account name	Amount £	Debit ✓	Credit ✓

(c) Record the net wages paid to the employees

Account name	Amount £	Debit ✓	Credit ✓

(d) Record the trade union liability

Account name	Amount £	Debit ✓	Credit ✓

Picklist:

Bank
Employees' NIC
Employer's NIC
HM Revenue and Customs
Income tax
Net wages
Trade union liability
Wages control
Wages expense

Errors and the trial balance

Learning outcomes

Having studied this chapter you will be able to:

2.3	**Identify the purpose of the journal**
	• Errors that are corrected through the journal and the effect on the trial balance: disclosed and not disclosed
	• Names of errors not disclosed by trial balance:
	– Errors of commission
	– Errors of omission
	– Errors of original entry
	– Errors of principle
	– Reversal of entries
	– Compensating errors
4.2	**Produce journal entries to correct errors not disclosed by the trial balance**
	• Correct errors using the journal:
	– Errors of commission
	– Errors of omission
	– Errors of original entry
	– Errors of principle
	– Reversal of entries
	– Compensating errors
4.3	**Produce journal entries to correct errors disclosed by the trial balance**
	• Open a suspense account
	• Correct errors and clear the suspense account using the journal
4.4	**Use journal entries to make adjustments in the ledger accounts**
	• Post journal entries to the general ledger accounts
	• Total and balance the general ledger accounts:
	– Balance carried down
	– Balance brought down
4.5	**Redraft the trial balance following adjustments**
	• Recalculate the balance of a general ledger account following journal entries
	• Complete a trial balance from adjusted and unadjusted balances
	• Balance the adjusted trial balance: total debit and credit columns

Assessment context

You will be given details of transactions which have been recorded incorrectly. You will be required to enter journals to remove the incorrect entry, record the correct entry and where relevant, clear the suspense account. Some tasks will ask you to redraft the trial balance following the correction of errors.

Qualification context

In the *Advanced bookkeeping* unit you may be asked to identify the cause of imbalances in the trial balance and take appropriate action to remedy them.

Business context

All businesses must be able to identify errors, and correct them in a timely, appropriate manner in order to prepare accurate, complete financial statements.

Chapter overview

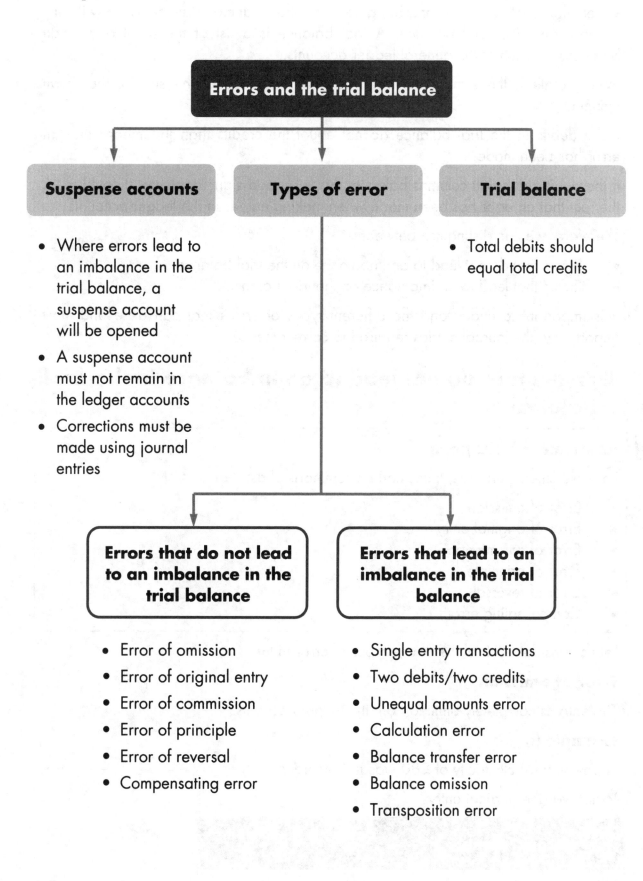

Errors and the trial balance

Suspense accounts

- Where errors lead to an imbalance in the trial balance, a suspense account will be opened
- A suspense account must not remain in the ledger accounts
- Corrections must be made using journal entries

Types of error

Trial balance

- Total debits should equal total credits

Errors that do not lead to an imbalance in the trial balance

- Error of omission
- Error of original entry
- Error of commission
- Error of principle
- Error of reversal
- Compensating error

Errors that lead to an imbalance in the trial balance

- Single entry transactions
- Two debits/two credits
- Unequal amounts error
- Calculation error
- Balance transfer error
- Balance omission
- Transposition error

Introduction

When the bookkeeper is preparing to draft the financial statements he will first prepare an initial trial balance. A trial balance is a list of the debit and credit balances on each of the general ledger accounts.

When totalled, the sum of the debit column should equal the sum of the credit column.

If the debits in the trial balance do not equal the credits than this means that an error has been made.

If the debit and credit columns balance, this is a good sign. However, it could mask the fact that an error has been made when making entries in the ledger accounts.

Therefore, we can distinguish between:

- Errors that do not lead to an imbalance on the trial balance
- Errors that lead to an imbalance on the trial balance

It is important to understand the different types of errors that can arise and most importantly, the journal entries required to correct them.

1 Errors that do not lead to an imbalance in the trial balance

> **Assessment focus point**
>
> For assessment purposes, these can be summarised as:
>
> - Error of omission
> - Error of original entry
> - Error of commission
> - Error of principle
> - Error of reversal
> - Compensating error

Let us consider each of the above types of error in turn.

Error of omission

The entry is completely omitted from the ledger accounts.

Example (i)

A payment for electricity of £80 was not recorded.

What was the original entry?

Account name	Debit £	Credit £
Electricity	Nil	
Bank		nil

What should the entry have been?

Account name	Debit £	Credit £
Electricity	80	
Bank		80

Record the journal to correct the error.

Account name	Debit £	Credit £
Electricity	80	
Bank		80

Error of original entry

When an entry has been made so that debits = credits but the amount is incorrect.

Example (ii)

A payment of £520 from a credit customer is recorded as £250.

What was the original entry?

Account name	Debit £	Credit £
Bank	250	
Sales ledger control		250

What should the entry have been?

Account name	Debit £	Credit £
Bank	520	
Sales ledger control		520

Record the journal to:

(a) Remove the incorrect entries

Account name	Debit £	Credit £
Sales ledger control	250	
Bank		250

(b) Record the correct entries

Account name	Debit £	Credit £
Bank	520	
Sales ledger control		520

Note that in practice errors are often corrected by posting the difference to the account affected. However, in the assessment you are required to first remove the incorrect entry and then record the correct entry, as is shown here.

Error of commission

The double entry is arithmetically correct but a wrong account of the same type has been used.

Example (iii)

The wages and salaries expense account is incorrectly debited with a rent expense of £100.

What was the original entry?

Account name	Debit £	Credit £
Wages and salaries expense	100	
Bank		100

What should the entry have been?

Account name	Debit £	Credit £
Rent	100	
Bank		100

Record the journal to correct the error.

Account name	Debit £	Credit £
Rent	100	
Wages and salaries expense		100

Error of principle

This is similar to an error of commission, but this time the wrong type of account has been used. A posting is made to a statement of profit or loss (SPL) account instead of a statement of financial position (SOFP) account or vice versa.

When the company accounts are prepared, both the SPL and SOFP will be incorrect (unless the error is detected and corrected).

Example (iv)

A motor vehicle petrol expense of £40 is debited to the non-current asset motor vehicles account instead of being expensed to the statement of profit or loss.

What was the original entry?

Account name	Debit £	Credit £
Motor vehicles (SOFP)	40	
Bank		40

What should the entry have been?

Account name	Debit £	Credit £
Motor vehicles expense (SPL)	40	
Bank		40

Record the journal to correct the error.

Account name	Debit £	Credit £
Motor vehicles expense (SPL)	40	
Motor vehicles (SOFP)		40

Error of reversal

The debit and credit entries are on the wrong side of the respective accounts.

Example (v)

The entries to record a sale on credit of £160 were included on the wrong side of the respective accounts.

What was the original entry?

Account name	Debit £	Credit £
Sales	160	
Sales ledger control		160

What should the entry have been?

Account name	Debit £	Credit £
Sales ledger control	160	
Sales		160

Record the journal to:

(a) Remove the incorrect entries

Account name	Debit £	Credit £
Sales		160
Sales ledger control	160	

(b) Record the correct entries

Account name	Debit £	Credit £
Sales ledger control	160	
Sales		160

Compensating error

This is where two errors are made which exactly cancel each other out. The errors are unrelated but the fact that they both occurred will mean that there is no imbalance in the trial balance to help identify them. (These are rare in practice.)

Example (vi)

The sales ledger control account was incorrectly debited with £4,100 in respect of a sales transaction. The correct amount of £4,000 was credited to the sales account.

The purchases returns account was incorrectly credited with £1,600 in respect of a purchases returns transaction. The correct amount of £1,500 was debited to the purchases ledger control account.

What was the original entry?

Account name	Debit £	Credit £
Sales ledger control	4,100	
Sales		4,000
Purchases ledger control	1,500	
Purchases returns		1,600

What should the entry have been?

Account name	Debit £	Credit £
Sales ledger control	4,000	
Sales		4,000
Purchases ledger control	1,500	
Purchases returns		1,500

Record the journal to correct the errors.

Account name	Debit £	Credit £
Sales ledger control	4,000	
Sales ledger control		4,100
Purchases returns	1,600	
Purchases returns		1,500

2 Errors that lead to an imbalance in the trial balance

Errors that lead to an imbalance in the trial balance can be summarised as:

- Single entry transactions
- Two debits/two credits
- Unequal amounts error
- Calculation error
- Balance transfer error
- Balance omission
- Transposition error

Where these errors occur, in the initial trial balance total debits will not equal total credits. Therefore, a suspense account is opened to make the trial balance totals equal.

The suspense account must **not** remain in the ledger accounts. The reasons for the imbalance on the trial balance must be investigated and corrections made using journal entries. Once the corrections have been put through, the suspense account will be cleared to a balance of zero.

The steps to follow to identify and correct errors are to:

- Identify what the incorrect double entry was
- Determine what the correct double entry should have been

- Prepare the journal entries to:
  - Reverse the incorrect double entry
  - Make the correct double entry

The illustration below shows several errors which have led to an imbalance in the trial balance. At the start of the illustration the suspense account is opened. The journals required to correct the errors are then processed and by the end of the illustration, the balance on the suspense account has been cleared.

This is longer than an assessment-standard task and demonstrates the principles you need to understand with regard to clearing a suspense account balance.

Note that for each of the examples, when we ask 'What was the original entry?', we are considering the journals that would have been made by the bookkeeper. If there is an imbalance in the journal entries, by default the balancing figure (β) will go to the suspense account.

Illustration 1: Errors that lead to an imbalance in the trial balance

A business drafted its initial trial balance and found the totals of the debit and credit columns were as follows:

Account name	Debit £	Credit £
Trial balance totals (initial)	150,500	160,000

The difference of £9,500 is initially dealt with by opening a suspense account to create a balanced trial balance.

Account name	Debit £	Credit £
Trial balance totals (initial)	150,500	160,000
Suspense	9,500	
Trial balance totals	160,000	160,000

The trial balance now balances but there is also a temporary new general ledger account, the suspense account, with a debit balance.

Suspense

Details	Amount £	Details	Amount £
Balance b/f	9,500		

The following errors are identified:

Single entry transactions

One side of the double entry has been made (eg the debit and not the credit).

Example (i)

A wages and salaries transaction of £4,482 is only recorded in the wages and salaries control account. The entry to the wages and salaries expense account is omitted.

What was the original entry?

Account name	Debit £	Credit £
Wages and salaries expense	0	
Suspense β	4,482	
Wages and salaries control		4,482

What should the entry have been?

Account name	Debit £	Credit £
Wages and salaries expense	4,482	
Wages and salaries control		4,482

Record the journal to correct the error.

Account name	Debit £	Credit £
Wages and salaries expense	4,482	
Suspense		4,482

Two debits/two credits

Both accounts have been posted with debit entries or both accounts have been posted with credit entries.

Example (ii)

An electricity payment of £2,500 is credited to both nominal ledger accounts.

What was the original entry?

Account name	Debit £	Credit £
Suspense β	5,000	
Electricity expense		2,500
Bank		2,500

What should the entry have been?

Account name	Debit £	Credit £
Electricity expense	2,500	
Bank		2,500

Record the journal to correct the error.

Account name	Debit £	Credit £
Electricity expense	2,500	
Electricity expense	2,500	
Suspense		5,000

Unequal amounts error

One side of the double entry is made accurately but an error is made in the other side.

Example (iii)

A rent payment was correctly posted to the rent expense account as £1,100 but incorrectly posted to the bank account as £1,000.

What was the original entry?

Account name	Debit £	Credit £
Rent expense	1,100	
Bank		1,000
Suspense β		100

What should the entry have been?

Account name	Debit £	Credit £
Rent expense	1,100	
Bank		1,100

Record the journal to correct the error.

Account name	Debit £	Credit £
Suspense	100	
Bank		100

Calculation error

A mistake is made when calculating the balance on a ledger account.

Example (iv)

The sales ledger control account has not been correctly balanced. It should show £1,200 on the sales ledger control account instead of £700. The corresponding credit entries were correctly included in the trial balance.

What was the original entry?

Account name	Debit £	Credit £
Sales ledger control	700	
Suspense β	500	

What should the entry have been?

Account name	Debit £	Credit £
Sales ledger control	1,200	

Record the journal to correct the error.

Account name	Debit £	Credit £
Sales ledger control	500	
Suspense		500

Balance transfer error

A balance on a general ledger account is transferred incorrectly into the trial balance.

Example (v)

A balance on the petty cash account was included in the trial balance as £600. It should have been £550. The corresponding credit entries were correctly included in the trial balance.

What was the original entry?

Account name	Debit £	Credit £
Petty cash account in the TB	600	
Suspense β		50

What should the entry have been?

Account name	Debit £	Credit £
Petty cash account in the TB	550	

Record the journal to correct the error.

Account name	Debit £	Credit £
Suspense	50	
Petty cash account in the TB		50

Balance omission

A balance on the ledger account is omitted from the trial balance.

Example (vi)

The discounts received balance of £350 was unintentionally excluded from the trial balance. The corresponding debit balance was correctly included in the main ledger.

What was the original entry?

Account name	Debit £	Credit £
Discounts received in the TB		0
Suspense β		350

What should the entry have been?

Account name	Debit £	Credit £
Discount received in the TB		350

Record the journal to correct the error.

Account name	Debit £	Credit £
Suspense	350	
Discounts received in the TB		350

Transposition error

The digits in a number are transposed (swapped round) in:

- One general ledger account (eg debit entry) or

- The balance on a general ledger account when it is taken to the trial balance

Note that if a transposition error has occurred, the difference between total debits and total credits is exactly divisible by nine. This is a useful trick to know when identifying errors.

Example (vii)

A purchases return is recorded correctly in the purchase ledger control account as £402 but incorrectly in purchases returns as £420.

What was the original entry?

Account name	Debit £	Credit £
Purchases ledger control	402	
Purchases returns		420
Suspense β	18	

What should the entry have been?

Account name	Debit £	Credit £
Purchases ledger control	402	
Purchases returns		402

Record the journal to correct the error.

Account name	Debit £	Credit £
Purchases returns	18	
Suspense		18

The suspense account will be cleared by posting the journals to correct the error which refer to the suspense account:

Suspense

Details	Amount £	Details	Amount £
Balance b/f	9,500	Wages and salaries expense (i)	4,482
Bank (iii)	100	Electricity expense (ii)	5,000
Petty cash account in the TB (v)	50	Sales ledger control (iv)	500
Discounts received in the TB (vi)	350	Purchases returns (viii)	18
	10,000		10,000

The suspense account now stands at nil as there is no balance c/d after the relevant entries have been made. This shows that the errors have been corrected. A redrafted trial balance could now be prepared.

3 Errors and the trial balance

It is important to understand the types of errors that are disclosed by the trial balance and those that are not. We will test your knowledge of this topic in the next activity.

As you are working through this example, consider the trial balance totals. Will the error you are addressing cause an imbalance in the totals?

BPP
LEARNING MEDIA

Activity 1: Errors and the trial balance

Required

Show which of the errors below are, or are not, disclosed by the trial balance.

Error in the general ledger	Error disclosed by the trial balance √	Error NOT disclosed by the trial balance √
Recording a receipt of bank interest on the debit side of both the bank and bank interest accounts	√	
Recording a payment for a motor vehicle in the motor expenses account		
Recording a purchases credit note on the credit side of the purchases ledger control account and the debit side of the purchases returns account		√
Incorrectly calculating the balance on the wages and salaries account	√	
Recording a receipt by cheque from a customer in the bank account and sales ledger only	√	
Recording a bank payment of £510 for electricity as £5,100 in both accounts		√

4 Opening a suspense account

If an initial trial balance does not balance, you may need to open a suspense account. The steps are:

1. Find the difference between the total of the debit and total of the credit columns

2. Include the difference in the column with the lower (draft) total, so that if you were preparing a trial balance, the two sides balance

Activity 2: Opening a suspense account

Bee's trial balance was extracted and did not balance. The debit column of the trial balance totalled £390,200 and the credit column totalled £380,400.

Required

What entry would be made in the suspense account to balance the trial balance?

Account name	Amount £	Debit √	Credit √
Suspense			

5 Identifying and correcting errors

Remember, the steps to follow to identify and correct errors are to:

- Identify what the incorrect double entry was

- Determine what the correct double entry should have been

- Prepare the journal entries to:
    - Reverse the incorrect double entry
    - Make the correct double entry

Activity 3: Identifying and correcting errors

Julian's initial trial balance includes a suspense account with a balance of £150.

The error has been traced to the sales returns day book shown below.

Sales returns day book

Date 20XX	Details	Credit note number	Total £	VAT £	Net £
31 Jan	Brian	208	672	112	560
31 Jan	Elsie	209	4,200	700	3,500
31 Jan	Simon	210	3,384	564	2,820
	Totals		8,256 √	1,526	6,880 √

Required

Set-up for part (a) (note – this does not form part of an exam standard answer)

162

What was the original entry?

Account name	Amount £	Debit √	Credit √
Sales LGA	8256		√
Sales returns	6880	√	
VAT	1526	√	
Suspense	150		√

What should the entry have been?

Account name	Amount £	Debit √	Credit √
SLCA	8256		√
Sales returns	6880	√	
VAT	1376	√	

(a) **Identify the error and record the journal entries needed in the general ledger to:**

(i)   Remove the incorrect entry

Account name	Amount £	Debit √	Credit √
VAT	1526		√

(ii)   Record the correct entry

Account name	Amount £	Debit √	Credit √
VAT	1376	√	

(iii)   Remove the suspense account balance

Account name	Amount £	Debit √	Credit √
Suspense	150	√	

Picklist:

Brian
Elsie
Purchases
Purchases ledger control
Purchases returns
Sales
Sales ledger control
Sales returns
Simon
Suspense
VAT

An entry to record a bank receipt from a credit customer for £4,400 has been reversed.

(b) Record the journal entries needed in the general ledger to:

(i) Remove the incorrect entry

Account name	Amount £	Debit ✓	Credit ✓
SLCA	4400		✓
Bank	4400	✓	

(ii) Record the correct entry

Account name	Amount £	Debit ✓	Credit ✓

Picklist:

Bank
Cash
Purchases
Purchases ledger control
Sales
Sales ledger control
Suspense
VAT

6 Posting journals to correct errors

Once the bookkeeper has noted the journals needed to correct errors in the accounting records, the journals need to be posted to the nominal ledger.

Here, you need to work down the list of journals, posting to them to the relevant nominal ledger account. Remember to include each entry on the correct side of the ledger accounts and cross-reference them appropriately.

Where there is a suspense account, once all the journal entries have been posted, the suspense account will stand at 'nil'.

Activity 4: Posting journals to the general ledger

The journal entries below have been prepared to correct errors.

Journal entries

Account name	Debit £	Credit £
Telephone	242	
Suspense		242
Suspense	2,200	
Purchases		2,200

Required

Post the journal entries to the general ledger accounts below. Total the accounts. Show the balance carried down in the telephone and purchase accounts.

Telephone

Details	Amount £	Details	Amount £
Balance b/f	1,872		
Bank	550		

Purchases

Details	Amount £	Details	Amount £
Balance b/f	4,300		
Purchases ledger control	11,100		

Suspense

Details	Amount £	Details	Amount £
		Balance b/f	1,958

Picklist:

Balance b/f
Balance c/d
Purchases
Suspense
Telephone

Redrafting the trial balance following the correction of errors

Earlier in the chapter we looked at opening a suspense account, to balance an initial trial balance.

When you are redrafting a trial balance following the correction of errors, the steps are as follows:

1.   Review the journal entries and note the balances that will change as a result of the journal entries.

2. Enter the unaffected numbers into the trial balance.

3. Process the journals given in the scenario. (You will need to do this on scrap paper and may like to set up T accounts to do this.) Once the journals are posted include the revised numbers in the trial balance.

4. Total the trial balance and include the totals in the debit and credit columns.

5. As a check that you have posted the entries correctly, the columns should now balance.

Activity 5: Redrafting the trial balance following the correction of errors

On 30 September, Molly Co extracted an initial trial balance which did not balance, and a suspense account was opened with a £18,874 debit balance. On 1 October journal entries were prepared to correct the errors that had been found, and clear the suspense account. The list of balances in the initial trial balance, and the journal entries to correct the errors, are shown below.

Required

Redraft the trial balance by placing the figures in the debit or credit column. You should take into account the journal entries that will clear the suspense account.

Journal entries

Account name	Debit £	Credit £
Bank	9,482	
Suspense		9,482
Bank	9,482	
Suspense		9,482

Account name	Debit £	Credit £
Purchases returns	2,431	
Suspense		2,431
Purchases returns		2,521
Suspense	2,521	

Account names	Balances extracted on 30 September £	Balances at 1 October Debit £	Credit £
Plant	54,824		
Equipment	28,424		
Inventory	15,392		
Bank (overdraft)	9,482		
Petty cash	200		
Sales ledger control	64,136		
Purchases ledger control	65,024		
VAT owing to HM Revenue & Customs	9,424		
Capital	20,000		
Sales	309,565		
Purchases	140,592		
Purchases returns	2,431		
Wages	75,302		
Motor expenses	504		
Office expenses	6,825		
Rent and rates	4,265		
Heat and light	1,100		
Insurance	247		
Miscellaneous expenses	5,241		
Totals			

Chapter summary

- Errors in the accounting records that do not cause an imbalance on the trial balance are:

  - Error of original entry
  - Error of omission
  - Error of commission
  - Error of principle
  - Error of reversal
  - Compensating error

- Once identified, draft journal entries to (i) reverse the incorrect entries and (ii) make the correct entries.

- Some errors in the accounting records cause an imbalance on the trial balance – these include:

  - Single entry transactions
  - Two debits/two credits
  - Unequal amounts error
  - Calculation error
  - Balance transfer error
  - Balance omission
  - Transposition error

- If the trial balance does not balance, set up a suspense account to make the debits equal to the credits.

- Once the errors have been found, for each one:

  - Work out what the original, incorrect double entry was (including suspense account entries) and what the correct double entry should be

  - Draft journal entries to (i) reverse the incorrect entries and (ii) post the correct entries

  - Enter the journals to clear the suspense account

  - Redraft the trial balance (where required)

Keywords

- **Balance omission:** A ledger account balance has been left out of the trial balance completely

- **Balance transfer error:** A balance on a general ledger account is transferred incorrectly into the trial balance

- **Calculation error:** A mistake is made in calculating the balance on a ledger account

- **Compensating error:** Two (or more) separate errors have been made that completely cancel each other out

- **Error of commission:** The double entry is arithmetically correct but one of the entries has been made to the wrong account, though an account of the correct type

- **Error of omission:** Both the debit and credit entries have been omitted from the ledger accounts

- **Error of original entry:** Both the debit and credit entries in the ledgers have been made at the wrong amount

- **Error of principle:** The double entry is arithmetically correct but one of the entries has been to the wrong type of account

- **Error of reversal:** The debit and credit entries have been reversed in the ledger accounts

- **Single entry error:** Only one side of the double entry has been made

- **Suspense account:** An account opened in order to make the balances on a trial balance equal while the reason for the imbalance is discovered and corrected

- **Transposition error:** The digits in a number are transposed (swapped round)

- **Two debits/two credits error:** Instead of a debit and a credit entry, either two debits or two credits have been made

- **Unequal amounts error:** Debit and credit entries have been made for different amounts

Activity answers

Activity 1: Errors and the trial balance

Show which of the errors below are, or are not, disclosed by the trial balance.

Error in the general ledger	Error disclosed by the trial balance √	Error NOT disclosed by the trial balance √
Recording a receipt of bank interest on the debit side of both the bank and bank interest accounts	√	
Recording a payment for a motor vehicle in the motor expenses account		√
Recording a purchases credit note on the credit side of the purchases ledger control account and the debit side of the purchases returns account		√
Incorrectly calculating the balance on the wages and salaries account	√	
Recording a receipt by cheque from a customer in the bank account and sales ledger only	√	
Recording a bank payment of £510 for electricity as £5,100 in both accounts		√

Although items 2, 3 and 6 are recorded incorrectly, both sides of the entries are for the same amount and therefore will not cause an imbalance in the trial balance.

However, item 1 is a two debit entry; as there is no corresponding credit entry, the trial balance will not balance. Likewise, in item 4 the balance on the wages and salaries account is incorrect; the corresponding entries will be for the correct amount, hence the difference leading to an imbalance in the trial balance.

For item 5 the debit entry for the bank receipt has been recorded in the general ledger but the credit entry has not been posted to the sales ledger control account, hence an imbalance. The entry to the subsidiary sales ledger does not affect the trial balance.

Activity 2: Opening a suspense account

What entry would be made in the suspense account to balance the trial balance?

Account name	Amount £	Debit √	Credit √
Suspense	9,800		√

In the initial trial balance the debit column total exceeds the credit column total by £9,800. Therefore, to temporarily balance the trial balance, a suspense account with a credit of £9,800 is opened.

Activity 3: Identifying and correcting errors

What was the original entry?

Account name	Amount £	Debit √	Credit √
Sales returns	6,880	√	
VAT	1,526	√	
Sales ledger control	8,256		√
Suspense	150		√

What should the entry have been?

Account name	Amount £	Debit √	Credit √
Sales returns	6,880	√	
VAT	1,376	√	
Sales ledger control	8,256		√

(a) **Identify the error and record the journal entries needed in the general ledger to:**

(i) Remove the incorrect entry

Account name	Amount £	Debit √	Credit √
VAT	1,526		√

(ii) Record the correct entry

Account name	Amount £	Debit √	Credit √
VAT	1,376	√	

(iii) Remove the suspense account balance

Account name	Amount £	Debit √	Credit √
Suspense	150	√	

(b) Record the journal entries needed in the general ledger to:

(i) Remove the incorrect entry

Account name	Amount £	Debit √	Credit √
Bank	4,400	√	
Sales ledger control	4,400		√

(ii) Record the correct entry

Account name	Amount £	Debit √	Credit √
Bank	4,400	√	
Sales ledger control	4,400		√

Activity 4: Posting journals to the general ledger

Post the journal entries to the general ledger accounts below. Total the accounts. Show the balance carried down in the telephone and purchase accounts.

Telephone

Details	Amount £	Details	Amount £
Balance b/f	1,872	Balance c/d	2,664
Bank	550		
Suspense	242		
	2,664		2,664

Purchases

Details	Amount £	Details	Amount £
Balance b/f	4,300	Suspense	2,200
Purchases ledger control	11,100	Balance c/d	13,200
	15,400		15,400

Suspense

Details	Amount £	Details	Amount £
Purchases	2,200	Balance b/f	1,958
		Telephone	242
	2,200		2,200

To post the journal entries work methodically down the list of debit and credit items given in the scenario. Ensure that you cross-reference them accurately between the T accounts. For example, the debit in the telephone T account of £242 must be cross-referenced to the credit in the suspense account of £242.

Activity 5: Redrafting the trial balance following the correction of errors

Redraft the trial balance by placing the figures in the debit or credit column. You should take into account the journal entries that will clear the suspense account.

Account names	Balances at 1 October Debit £	Credit £
Plant	54,824	
Equipment	28,424	
Inventory	15,392	
Bank	**9,482**	
Petty cash	200	
Sales ledger control	64,136	
Purchases ledger control		65,024
VAT owing to HM Revenue & Customs		9,424
Capital		20,000
Sales		309,565

Account names	Balances at 1 October Debit £	Credit £
Purchases	140,592	
Purchases returns		**2,521**
Wages	75,302	
Motor expenses	504	
Office expenses	6,825	
Rent and rates	4,265	
Heat and light	1,100	
Insurance	247	
Miscellaneous expenses	5,241	
Totals	406,534	406,534

Tutorial note

The journal entries to the suspense, bank and purchases returns accounts are as follows:

Suspense account

Details	Amount £	Details	Amount £
Balance b/d in the initial trial balance	18,874	Bank (to remove error to bank)	9,482
Purchases returns (to correctly include purchases returns)	2,521	Bank (to correctly include bank)	9,482
		Purchases returns (to remove error to purchases returns)	2,431
	21,395		21,395

Bank

Details	Amount £	Details	Amount £
Suspense (to remove error to bank)	9,482	Balance b/d in the initial trial balance	9,482
Suspense (to correctly include bank)	9,482	Balance c/d in the redrafted trial balance	9,482
	18,964		18,964
Balance b/d in the redrafted trial balance	9,482		

Purchases returns

Details	Amount £	Details	Amount £
Suspense (to remove error to purchases returns)	2,431	Balance b/d in the initial trial balance	2,431
Balance c/d in the redrafted trial balance	2,521	Suspense (to correctly include purchases returns)	2,521
	4,952		4,952
		Balance b/d in the redrafted trial balance	2,521

Test your learning

1   It is important to understand the types of error that are disclosed by the trial balance and those that are not.

Show which of the errors below are, or are not, disclosed by the trial balance.

Error in the general ledger	Error disclosed by the trial balance ✓	Error NOT disclosed by the trial balance ✓
Calculating the balance on a ledger account incorrectly by £100		
Recording a supplier's credit note for £800 at £80 in the purchases returns day book		
Forgetting to include a £200 balance for motor expenses in the trial balance		
Making the debit entry for a cash sale of £150 but not the credit entry		
Forgetting to record a petty cash payment of £20		
For a purchase of stationery on credit, debiting the PLCA and crediting the stationery account		

2   Alvescot Co's trial balance was extracted and did not balance. The debit column of the trial balance totalled £52,673 and the credit column totalled £61,920.

What entry would be made in the suspense account to balance the trial balance?

Account name	Amount £	Debit ✓	Credit ✓

3   An initial trial balance has a credit balance on the suspense account of £900. It was found that a receipt of £3,250 from a customer was recorded in the cash book correctly but in the sales ledger control account as £2,350.

Using the picklist, record the journal entries needed in the general ledger to:

(i)   Remove the amount entered incorrectly

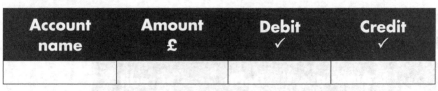

Account name	Amount £	Debit ✓	Credit ✓

(ii) Record the correct entry

Account name	Amount £	Debit ✓	Credit ✓

(iii) Remove the suspense account balance

Account name	Amount £	Debit ✓	Credit ✓

Picklist:

Bank
Sales ledger control
Suspense

4 The initial trial balance of a business includes a suspense account with a balance of £1,000.

The error has been traced to the casting of the net column of the purchases day book shown below.

Purchases day book

Date 20XX	Details	Invoice number	Total £	VAT £	Net £
31 Oct	Hughson Ltd	1902	1,740	290	1,450
31 Oct	Rundle Co	43902	432	72	360
31 Oct	Westcot Jenks	6327	2,562	427	2,135
	Totals		4,734	789	4,945

(a) Record the journal entries needed in the general ledger to:

(i) Remove the amount entered incorrectly

Account name	Amount £	Debit ✓	Credit ✓

(ii) Record the correct entry

Account name	Amount £	Debit ✓	Credit ✓

(iii) Remove the suspense account balance

Account name	Amount £	Debit ✓	Credit ✓

Picklist:

Purchases

Purchases ledger control

Suspense

(b) **An entry to record purchases of goods on credit for £980 (no VAT) has been reversed. Using the picklist, record the journal entries needed in the general ledger to:**

(i) Remove the incorrect entries

Account name	Amount £	Debit ✓	Credit ✓

(ii) Record the correct entries

Account name	Amount £	Debit ✓	Credit ✓

Picklist:

Bank

Purchases

Purchases ledger control

5   The initial trial balance of a business included a suspense account. All the bookkeeping errors have now been traced and the journal entries shown below have been recorded.

Journal entries

Account name	Debit £	Credit £
Discounts allowed	149	
Discounts received		149
Suspense	256	
Purchases		256
Motor expenses	893	
Suspense		893

Post the journal entries to the general ledger accounts.

Purchases

Details	Amount £	Details	Amount £

Motor expenses

Details	Amount £	Details	Amount £

Suspense

Details	Amount £	Details	Amount £
Balance b/f	637		

Discounts received

Details	Amount £	Details	Amount £

Discounts allowed

Details	Amount £	Details	Amount £

Picklist:

Balance b/f
Discounts allowed
Discounts received
Motor expenses
Purchases
Suspense

Test your learning: answers

Chapter 1

1

Statement	True ✓	False ✓
A bank draft cannot be cancelled once it has been issued.	✓	
Any customer who pays with a debit card is taking out a loan with its bank as a result.		✓

2

Statement	Impact on bank account
When a payment is made using a debit card, the money leaves the bank account	immediately
When a payment is made using a credit card, the money leaves the bank account	at a later date

3

Statement	Impact on bank account
When a payment is made using BACs direct credit, the money leaves the bank account	immediately
When a payment is made using CHAPS, the money leaves the bank account	immediately

4

Statement	Term
In respect of cheques, the person to whom the cheque is payable is the	payee
In respect of cheques, the person writing and signing the cheque in order to make the payment is the	drawer
In respect of cheques, the bank who has issued the cheque and will have to pay the cheque (ie the customer's bank) is the	drawee

5

| A | standing order | is a method of making the same regular payment for a fixed |

amount directly from a business's bank account to the bank account of a supplier.

Chapter 2

1   **If money is paid into a newly opened bank current account this will appear on the bank statement (tick the appropriate option):**

A debit entry	
A credit entry	✓

2   **If a figure for bank interest appeared in the paid in column of the bank statement, this would be adjusted for in the (tick the appropriate option):**

Debit side of the cash book	✓
Credit side of the cash book	

3   **A standing order payment is on the bank statement but has been omitted from the cash book. This should be adjusted for in the (tick the appropriate option):**

Debit side of the cash book	
Credit side of the cash book	✓

4   **How should this be dealt with in the bank reconciliation statement? (Tick the appropriate option):**

As an unpresented cheque	✓
As an outstanding lodgement	

5   **Cash book**

Date 20XX	Details	Bank £	Date 20XX	Cheque number	Details	Bank £
01 Feb	Balance b/f	6,230	01 Feb	003252	Jeggers Ltd	2,567
20 Feb	Straightens Co	2,228	01 Feb	003253	Short & Fell	333
21 Feb	Plumpers	925	01 Feb	003254	Rastop Ltd	1,006
22 Feb	Eastern Supplies	1,743	01 Feb	003255	A & D Trading	966
09 Feb	Branthill Co	1,559	02 Feb	003256	Jesmond Warr	2,309
			02 Feb	003257	Nistral Ltd	3,775
			13 Feb	003258	Simpsons	449
			13 Feb		AxDC	250
			18 Feb		DD Trust Insurance	325
			20 Feb		Bank charges	14
			22 Feb		Interest charge	56
			23 Feb		Balance c/d	635
		12,685				12,685
24 Feb	Balance b/d	635				

Bank reconciliation statement as at 23 Feb 20XX

Bank reconciliation statement	£
Balance per bank statement	725
Add:	
Pumpers	925
Eastern Supplies	1,743
Total to add	2,668
Less:	
Jesmond Warr	2,309
Simpsons	449
Total to subtract	2,758
Balance as per cash book	635

Chapter 3

1

Account name	Amount £	Debit √	Credit √
Sales returns	1,500	√	
VAT	300	√	
Sales ledger control	1,800		√

2

Account name	Amount £	Debit √	Credit √
Purchases ledger control	900	√	
VAT	150		√
Purchases returns	750		√

3 **General ledger**

Sales ledger control

Details	Amount £	Details	Amount £
Balance b/d	780.31	Bank	670.11
Sales	906.24	Balance c/d	1,016.44
	1,686.55		1,686.55
Balance b/d	1,016.44		

Sales ledger

Virgo Partners

Details	Amount £	Details	Amount £
Balance b/d	227.58	Bank	117.38
Invoice	96.72		
Invoice	214.44	Balance c/d	421.36
	538.74		538.74
Balance b/d	421.36		

McGowan & Sons

Details	Amount £	Details	Amount £
Balance b/d	552.73	Bank	552.73
Invoice	595.08	Balance c/d	595.08
	1,147.81		1,147.81
Balance b/d	595.08		

Reconciliation

	Amount £
Sales ledger control account balance as at 31 May	1,016.44
Total of sales ledger accounts as at 31 May (see workings)	1,016.44
Difference	0

Workings

	Amount £
Virgo Partners	421.36
McGowan & Sons	595.08
Total	1,016.44

4 General ledger

Purchases ledger control

Details	Amount £	Details	Amount £
Bank	744.68	Balance b/d	591.56
Balance c/d	824.40	Purchases	977.52
	1,569.08		1,569.08
		Balance b/d	824.40

Purchases ledger

Jenkins Suppliers

Details	Amount £	Details	Amount £
Bank	441.56	Balance b/d	441.56
Balance c/d	671.28	Invoice	219.96
		Invoice	451.32
	1,112.84		1,112.84
		Balance b/d	671.28

Kilnfarm Paper

Details	Amount £	Details	Amount £
Bank	150.00	Balance b/d	150.00
Bank	153.12	Invoice	153.12
Balance c/d	153.12	Invoice	153.12
	456.24		456.24
		Balance b/d	153.12

Reconciliation

	Amount £
Purchases ledger control account balance as at 31 May	824.40
Total of purchases ledger accounts as at 31 May (see workings)	824.40
Difference	0

Workings

	£
Jenkins Suppliers	671.28
Kilnfarm Paper	153.12
Total	824.40

5 **(a)**

VAT control

Details	Amount £	Details	Amount £
Purchases	14,368	Sales	29,072
Sales returns	858	Cash sales	332
		Purchases returns	488

(b)

	✓
Yes	
No	✓

The amount is owing **to** HMRC, not from HMRC. The total credits exceed the debits, therefore, there is a liability.

Chapter 4

1

Statement	True ✓	False ✓
An aged receivables analysis is a schedule showing, for each credit customer, how long the component parts of the balance have been unpaid.	✓	

2

Statements	√
The sales day book was undercast by £250 on one page.	
An invoice for £250 was omitted from the sales ledger account.	√
A discount allowed to a customer of £250 was posted to the debit side of the sales ledger account.	
Cash received of £250 was only posted to the sales ledger control account.	

Per the scenario, the sales ledger control account balance is higher then the total of the sales ledger account balances, therefore:

Statement 1 – this cannot be correct. In the event that the sales day book totals are undercast, the sales ledger control account would be lower than the total of the sales ledger balances

Statement 2 – this is correct as a debit balance of £250 has been omitted from the sales ledger, therefore it is lower than the control account by this amount

Statement 3 – this is incorrect as debit entries increase the sales ledger balances; therefore, if a discount allowed was posted to the debit side of the sales ledger account (but correctly entered in the control account), the sales ledger totals would be higher than the control account balance

Statement 4 – this is incorrect. If cash received is only omitted from the sales ledgers, the total of the ledger balances will be higher than the control account balance.

3

Account name	Amount £	Debit √	Credit √
Irrecoverable debt expenses	1,200	√	
VAT	240	√	
Sales ledger control	1,440		√

4

Account name	Amount £	Debit √	Credit √
Irrecoverable debts	1,290	√	
VAT	258	√	
Sales ledger control	1,548		√

5 **(a)**

Details	Amount £	Debit ✓	Credit ✓
Amount due to credit suppliers at 1 August	42,394		✓
Payments to credit suppliers	39,876	✓	
Purchases on credit	31,243		✓
Purchases returned to credit suppliers	1,266	✓	
Discounts received	501	✓	

(b)

	✓
Dr £31,994	
Cr £31,994	✓
Dr £34,526	
Cr £34,526	
Dr £32,996	
Cr £32,996	

(c)

	Amount £
Purchases ledger control account balance as at 31 August	31,994
Total of purchases ledger accounts as at 31 August	32,190
Difference	196

(d)

	✓
A debit balance in the purchases ledger may have been included as a credit balance when calculating the total of the list of balances	✓
A credit balance in the purchases ledger may have been included as a debit balance when calculating the total of the list of balances	
A credit note may have been omitted from the purchases returns day book total	
Discounts received may only have been entered in the purchases ledger	

The total of the subsidiary purchases ledger accounts exceeds the purchases ledger control account balance by £196.

Statement 1 – in the purchases ledger, credit entries increase the closing balance. Therefore, including a debit balance as a credit balance explains the difference.

Statement 2 – including a credit balance as a debit balance in the purchases ledger would result in the total of the purchases ledger account balances being lower than the purchases ledger control account balance, therefore this statement is incorrect.

Statements 3 and 4 – omitting credit note and discount received balances from the purchases ledger control account would result in the purchases ledger control account balance being higher than the total of the subsidiary purchases ledger accounts. This is not the case and therefore these statements are incorrect.

Chapter 5

1

Account name	Amount £	Debit ✓	Credit ✓
Capital	28,000		✓
Cash at bank	21,000	✓	
Loan from bank	5,000		✓
Machinery	12,000	✓	

2

£	1,642.84

Working

	Amount £
Gross pay (£27,000/12)	2,250.00
Income tax	(418.16)
Employee's NIC	(189.00)
Net pay	1,642.84

3

	Statutory deduction ✓	Voluntary deduction ✓
Pension contributions		✓
Income tax	✓	
Employee's NIC	✓	
Trade union fees		✓

4

	True ✓	False ✓
Employer's NIC are deducted from gross pay.		✓
Employer's pension contributions are in addition to gross pay.	✓	

5 **(a)**

Account name	Amount £	Debit ✓	Credit ✓
Wages expense	13,776	✓	
Wages control	13,776		✓

Working: £12,756 + £1,020 = £13,776

(b)

Account name	Amount £	Debit ✓	Credit ✓
Wages control	3,698	✓	
HM Revenue & Customs	3,698		✓

Working: £1,020 + £765 + £1,913 = £3,698

(c)

Account name	Amount £	Debit ✓	Credit ✓
Wages control	9,978	✓	
Bank	9,978		✓

Working: £12,756 – £1,913 – £765 – £100 = £9,978

(d)

Account name	Amount £	Debit ✓	Credit ✓
Wages control	100	✓	
Trade union liability	100		✓

Chapter 6

1

Error in the general ledger	Error disclosed by the trial balance ✓	Error NOT disclosed by the trial balance ✓
Calculating the balance on a ledger account incorrectly by £100	✓	
Recording a supplier's credit note for £800 at £80 in the purchases returns day book		✓
Forgetting to include a £200 balance for motor expenses in the trial balance	✓	
Making the debit entry for a cash sale of £150 but not the credit entry	✓	
Forgetting to record a petty cash payment of £20		✓
For a purchase of stationery on credit, debiting the PLCA and crediting the stationery account		✓

Statement 1 – the debit and credit entries differ by £100; this will be disclosed by the trial balance

Statement 2 – the amount is incorrect, however, the amount posted is the same on the debit and credit sides, therefore, this will not be disclosed by the trial balance

Statement 3 – the debit and credit column totals differ by £200 in respect of this transaction, therefore, the trial balance will not balance

Statement 4 – only the debit entry relating to this cash sale has been posted; the credit entry has not been posted and therefore the trial balance will not balance

Statement 5 – the item is omitted, therefore, the trial balance will still balance

Statement 6 – the debit and credit entries have been reversed and are therefore incorrect, however, they are equal and so the trial balance will still balance

2

Account name	Amount £	Debit ✓	Credit ✓
Suspense	9,247	✓	

3 **(i) Remove the amount entered incorrectly.**

Account name	Amount £	Debit ✓	Credit ✓
Sales ledger control	2,350	✓	

(ii) Record the correct entry.

Account name	Amount £	Debit ✓	Credit ✓
Sales ledger control	3,250		✓

(iii) Remove the suspense account balance.

Account name	Amount £	Debit ✓	Credit ✓
Suspense	900	✓	

4 **(a) (i)**

Account name	Amount £	Debit ✓	Credit ✓
Purchases	4,945		✓

(ii)

Account name	Amount £	Debit ✓	Credit ✓
Purchases	3,945	✓	

(iii)

Account name	Amount £	Debit ✓	Credit ✓
Suspense	1,000	✓	

(b) (i)

Account name	Amount £	Debit ✓	Credit ✓
Purchases	980	✓	
Purchases ledger control	980		✓

(ii)

Account name	Amount £	Debit ✓	Credit ✓
Purchases	980	✓	
Purchases ledger control	980		✓

5

Purchases

Details	Amount £	Details	Amount £
		Suspense	256

Motor expenses

Details	Amount £	Details	Amount £
Suspense	893		

Suspense

Details	Amount £	Details	Amount £
Balance b/f	637	Motor expenses	893
Purchases	256		

Discounts received

Details	Amount £	Details	Amount £
		Discounts allowed	149

Discounts allowed

Details	Amount £	Details	Amount £
Discounts received	149		

198

Synoptic assessment preparation

Certain *Bookkeeping controls* assessment objectives will be tested in the *AAT foundation certificate in accounting* synoptic assessment. Therefore, at this stage in your studies, it is useful to consider the style of tasks you may see in the synoptic assessment.

However, it is recommended that the *AAT foundation certificate in accounting* synoptic assessment is only taken when all other units have been completed.

Questions

1

It is the end of July and you have a partially prepared the sales ledger control account, as shown below.

Sales ledger account

Details	Amount £	Details	Amount £
Balance b/f	51,250	Bank	43,450
		Irrecoverable debt	2,300

You now have the totals of the sales and sales returns day books and must record the appropriate amounts in the sales ledger control account.

Sales day book (extract)

Date 20XX	Details	Total £	VAT £	Net £
31 Jul	Totals	50,640	8,440	42,200

Sales returns day book (extract)

Date 20XX	Details	Total £	VAT £	Net £
31 Jul	Totals	3,720	620	3,100

(a) What will be the entries in the sales ledger control account?

Account name	Amount £	Debit √	Credit √
Entry from the sales day book			
Entry from the sales returns day book			

(b) What will be the balance carried down on the sales ledger control account?

Amount £	Debit √	Credit √

Your next task is to reconcile the purchases ledger with the purchases ledger control account. These are the balances in the purchases ledger on 1 August.

Credit suppliers	Balances	
	Amount £	Debit/Credit
W Griffin	24,200	Credit
G George	16,340	Credit
Philpot plc	550	Debit
Higgins and Co	3,540	Credit
Penny Ltd	7,470	Credit

You have inserted the balance of the purchases ledger control account in the reconciliation statement below.

(c) Complete the reconciliation statement by:
- **Inserting the total of the balances in the purchases ledger**
- **Calculating any difference**

Reconciliation statement	Amount £
Purchases ledger control account balance as at 1 August 20XX	51,800
Total of purchases ledger accounts as at 1 August 20XX	
Difference	

Your manager wants to know what may have caused the difference shown in the reconciliation statement.

(d) Which TWO of the reasons below could explain the difference you calculated in (c) above?

Reasons	√
A credit note was entered twice in the purchases ledger control account.	
An invoice was entered twice in a supplier's account in the purchases ledger.	
A payment was entered twice in a supplier's account in the purchases ledger.	
A discount received was entered twice in the purchases ledger control account.	
An invoice was entered twice in the purchases ledger control account.	
A discount received was not entered in a supplier's account in the purchases ledger.	

The list of balances in the purchases ledger above shows the account of Philpot plc has a debit balance. Your colleague has prepared a draft letter to be sent to Miss Kearns at Philpot plc requesting a cheque.

(e) Review the draft letter and highlight SIX errors. Errors may be wrongly spelt, incorrectly used or technically incorrect.

Dear Mr Kearns

Our purchases ledger shows an erroneous overpayment made earlier in the year has resulted in an amount of £450 owing to us. We would be grateful if you could confirm agreement of this aount and provide us with a bank transfer so that we can correct the error in preparation for our year end. If you require me to provide further details of the underpayment please do not hesitate to contact me and I will be happy to forward documentation to you.

Many thanks in anticipation of your co-operation in this manager.

Yours sincerely

2

You are preparing for the accounting month end at your company.

Your first task is to transfer data from the purchases day book to the ledgers. An extract from the purchases day book is shown below.

Purchases day book (extract)

Date 20XX	Details	Invoice number	Total £	VAT £	Net £
31 Sep	Jeremy Ltd	J3423	504	84	420

(a) Show whether the entries in the general ledger will be debit or credit entries.

Account name	Debit £	Credit £

(b) What will be the entry in the purchases ledger?

Account name	Debit £	Credit £

Picklist:

Jeremy Ltd
Purchases
Purchases ledger control
Purchases returns
VAT

You have found an error in the accounting records. A cheque payment of £5,230 to a credit supplier has been recorded as £5,320.

You have partially prepared journal entries to correct the error in the general ledger.

(c) Complete the journals below by:

- **Removing the incorrect entries, and**
- **Recording the correct entries**

Do not enter a zero in unused debit or credit column cells.

Journal to remove the incorrect entries

Account name	Debit £	Credit £
Bank		
Purchases ledger control		

Journal to record the correct entries

Account name	Debit £	Credit £
Purchases ledger control		
Bank		

You have also identified that discounts allowed were omitted from the general ledger. You have prepared the journal entries below to correct the omission.

Journal

Account name	Debit £	Credit £
Discounts allowed	300	
Sales ledger control		300

(d) Record the journal in the general ledger.

Discount allowed

Details	Amount £	Details	Amount £
Balance b/f	2,100		

Sales ledger account

Details	Amount £	Details	Amount £
Balance b/f	23,000		

3

On 31 August there is a debit bank balance in the cash book of £4,500. The bank statement on the same day shows cash in the bank of £6,455.

The bank statement has been checked against the cash book and the following items have been identified as unmatched:

Items on the bank statement

- BACS receipt from a credit customer, L Johnson, of £1,115

Items in cash book

- Cheque payment to a credit supplier, J William, of £840.

(a) What entry is required to update the cash book?

Picklist:

Debit bank with £840
Credit bank with £840
Debit bank with £1,115
Credit bank with £1,115

(b) Calculate the amount of the updated cash book balance.

£	

(c) Complete the bank reconciliation statement as at 31 August

Bank reconciliation statement as at 31 August 20XX	£
Balance as per bank statement	
Balance as per cash book	

Picklist:

Add: J William
Add: L Johnson
Less: J William
Less: L Johnson

(d) Will the BACs receipt from L Johnson be a debit or credit entry in the sales ledger control account?

	√
Debit	
Credit	

Solutions

1

(a) What will be the entries in the sales ledger control account?

Account name	Amount £	Debit √	Credit √
Entry from the sales day book	50,640	√	
Entry from the sales returns day book	3,720		√

(b) What will be the balance carried down on the sales ledger control account?

Amount £	Debit √	Credit √
52,420		√

Working

Sales ledger account

Details	Amount £	Details	Amount £
Balance b/f	51,250	Bank	43,450
Sales	50,640	Irrecoverable debt	2,300
		Sales returns	3,720
		Balance c/d	52,420
	101,890		101,890

(c) Complete the reconciliation statement by:

- **Inserting the total of the balances in the purchases ledger**
- **Calculating any difference**

Reconciliation statement	Amount £
Purchases ledger control account balance as at 1 August 20XX	51,800
Total of purchases ledger accounts as at 1 August 20XX	51,000
Difference	800

(d) **Which TWO of the reasons below could explain the difference you calculated in (c) above?**

Reasons	√
A credit note was entered twice in the purchases ledger control account.	
An invoice was entered twice in a supplier's account in the purchases ledger.	
A payment was entered twice in a supplier's account in the purchases ledger.	√
A discount received was entered twice in the purchases ledger control account.	
An invoice was entered twice in the purchases ledger control account.	√
A discount received was not entered in a supplier's account in the purchases ledger.	

(e) **Review the draft letter and highlight SIX errors. Errors may be wrongly spelt, incorrectly used or technically incorrect.**

Dear Mr Kearns

Our purchases ledger shows an erroneous overpayment made earlier in the year has resulted in an amount of £450 owing to us. We would be grateful if you could confirm agreement of this aount and provide us with a bank transfer so that we can correct the error in preparation for our year end. If you require me to provide further details of the underpayment please do not hesitate to contact me and I will be happy to forward documentation to you.

Many thanks in anticipation of your co-operation in this manager.

Yours sincerely

Note – the correct wording is:

Dear Miss Kearns

Our purchases ledger shows an erroneous overpayment made earlier in the year has resulted in an amount of £550 owing to us. We would be grateful if you could confirm agreement of this amount and provide us with a cheque so that we can correct the error in preparation for our year end. If you require me to provide further details of the overpayment please do not hesitate to contact me and I will be happy to forward documentation to you.

Many thanks in anticipation of your co-operation in this matter.

Yours sincerely

2

(a) Show whether the entries in the general ledger will be debit or credit entries.

Account name	Debit £	Credit £
Purchases	420	
VAT	84	
Purchases ledger control		504

(b) What will be the entry in the purchases ledger?

Account name	Debit £	Credit £
Jeremy Ltd		504

(c) Complete the journals below by:

- **Removing the incorrect entries, and**
- **Recording the correct entries**

Journal to remove the incorrect entries

Account name	Debit £	Credit £
Bank	5,320	
Purchases ledger control		5,320

Journal to record the correct entries

Account name	Debit £	Credit £
Purchases ledger control	5,230	
Bank		5,230

(d)   Record the journal in the general ledger.

Discounts allowed

Details	Amount £	Details	Amount £
Balance b/f	2,100		
Sales ledger control	300		

Sales ledger account

Details	Amount £	Details	Amount £
Balance b/f	23,000	Discounts allowed	300

3

(a)   What entry is required to update the cash book?

Debit bank with £1,115

(b)   Calculate the amount of the updated cash book balance.

£	5,615

Working:

£4,500 + £1,115 = £5,615

(c)   Complete the bank reconciliation statement as at 31 August.

Bank reconciliation statement as at 31 August 20XX	£
Balance as per bank statement	6,455
Less: J William	840
Balance as per cash book	5,615

(d)   Will the BACs receipt from L Johnson be a debit or credit entry in the sales ledger control account?

	√
Debit	
Credit	√

The BACs receipt from L Johnson reduces the balance in the sales ledger control account as the customer is settling an amount that was owed. A decrease to the sales ledger control account is recorded as a credit entry to the account.

Glossary of terms

It is useful to be familiar with interchangeable terminology including IFRS and UK GAAP (generally accepted accounting principles).

Below is a short list of the most important terms you are likely to use or come across, together with their international and UK equivalents.

UK term	International term
Profit and loss account	**Statement of profit or loss (or statement of profit or loss and other comprehensive income)**
Turnover or Sales	Revenue or Sales revenue
Operating profit	Profit from operations
Reducing balance depreciation	Diminishing balance depreciation
Depreciation/depreciation expense(s)	Depreciation charge(s)
Balance sheet	**Statement of financial position**
Fixed assets	Non-current assets
Net book value	Carrying amount
Tangible assets	Property, plant and equipment
Stocks	Inventories
Trade debtors or Debtors	Trade receivables
Prepayments	Other receivables
Debtors and prepayments	Trade and other receivables
Cash at bank and in hand	Cash and cash equivalents
Long-term liabilities	Non-current liabilities
Trade creditors or creditors	Trade payables
Accruals	Other payables
Creditors and accruals	Trade and other payables
Capital and reserves	Equity (limited companies)
Profit and loss balance	Retained earnings
Cash flow statement	**Statement of cash flows**

Accountants often have a tendency to use several phrases to describe the same thing! Some of these are listed below:

Different terms for the same thing
Nominal ledger, main ledger or general ledger
Subsidiary ledgers, memorandum ledgers
Subsidiary (sales) ledger, sales ledger
Subsidiary (purchases) ledger, purchases ledger

Bibliography

The Association of Accounting Technicians (2016) [Online] Available from: https://www.aat.org.uk [Accessed 12 May 2016].

Index

A

Aged trade receivables analysis, 105

B

BACS direct credit, 11, 15, 24
Balance omission, 158, 170
Balance transfer error, 158, 170
Bank draft, 8, 15
Bank reconciliation, 26
Bank reconciliation statement, 43
Bank statement, 15, 43

C

Calculation error, 157, 170
CHAPS, 11, 15
Cheque, 5, 15
Clearing system, 15
Compensating error, 152, 170
Control account, 60, 79
Counter credit, 15, 25
Credit card, 7, 15
Credit control, 100

D

Debit card, 6, 15
Direct debit, 9, 15, 24
Discounts allowed, 59
Discounts received, 59
Dishonoured cheque, 6, 15
Drawee, 15
Drawer, 5, 15

E

Employees' national insurance contributions, 121, 136
Employer's national insurance contribution, 122, 136
Error of commission, 150, 170
Error of omission, 148, 170
Error of original entry, 149, 170
Error of principle, 150, 170
Error of reversal, 151, 170

F

Faster payments, 12, 15

G

Gross pay, 121, 125, 136

H

Her Majesty's Revenue & Customs (HMRC), 124, 136

I

Income tax, 121, 136
Irrecoverable debt, 101, 105

J

Journal book, 136
Journal entry, 117, 136

N

Net pay, 122, 125, 136

O

Outstanding lodgements, 43
Overdraft, 43

P

Payee, 15
Paying-in slip, 15
Payroll, 121
Payroll transactions, 136
Pension, 124
Pension contribution, 136
Prompt payment discounts, 59
Purchases ledger, 69, 79
Purchases ledger control, 56, 62, 79
Purchases ledger control account reconciliation, 105

R

Reconciliation, 66, 70

Notes

BPP
LEARNING MEDIA

REVIEW FORM

How have you used this Course Book?
(Tick one box only)

☐ Self study

☐ On a course_____

☐ Other _____

Why did you decide to purchase this Course Book? *(Tick one box only)*

☐ Have used BPP materials in the past

☐ Recommendation by friend/colleague

☐ Recommendation by a college lecturer

☐ Saw advertising

☐ Other _____

During the past six months do you recall seeing/receiving either of the following?
(Tick as many boxes as are relevant)

☐ Our advertisement in Accounting Technician

☐ Our Publishing Catalogue

Which (if any) aspects of our advertising do you think are useful?
(Tick as many boxes as are relevant)

☐ Prices and publication dates of new editions

☐ Information on Course Book content

☐ Details of our free online offering

☐ None of the above

Your ratings, comments and suggestions would be appreciated on the following areas of this Course Book.

	Very useful	Useful	Not useful
Chapter overviews	☐	☐	☐
Introductory section	☐	☐	☐
Quality of explanations	☐	☐	☐
Illustrations	☐	☐	☐
Chapter activities	☐	☐	☐
Test your learning	☐	☐	☐
Keywords	☐	☐	☐

	Excellent	Good	Adequate	Poor
Overall opinion of this Course Book	☐	☐	☐	☐

Do you intend to continue using BPP Products?   ☐ Yes ☐ No

Please note any further comments and suggestions/errors on the reverse of this page and return it to: Nisar Ahmed, AAT Head of Programme, BPP Learning Media Ltd, FREEPOST, London, W12 8AA.

Alternatively, the Head of Programme of this edition can be emailed at: nisarahmed@bpp.com

REVIEW FORM (continued)

TELL US WHAT YOU THINK

Please note any further comments and suggestions/errors below